CW01333035

TREASURE HUNTING THE
FLEA MARKETS
OF FRANCE

Typical collection of finds from a single flea market expedition May 2015

The essential guide to buying antiques
and collectables in France
Tony Collins

© 2015 by Tony Collins

All rights reserved. No part of this book may be reproduced, stored in a retrieval system or transmitted in any form without the permission of the author.

To Lydia for her valued advice and Jill, my companion on all those flea market expeditions.

CONTENTS

INTRODUCTION 7

CHAPTER   1 Flea markets and Vide greniers   10

CHAPTER   2 Lighting the home. Candlesticks & lanterns   20

CHAPTER   3 Pewter   27

CHAPTER   4 Silver and white metal   33

CHAPTER   5 Delft and Faïence pottery   39

CHAPTER   6 Glass   48

CHAPTER   7 Mediaeval woodcarvings   53

CHAPTER   8 The Church and objects of devotion   58

CHAPTER   9 Mediaeval manuscripts and paintings   64

CHAPTER   10 Furniture in the French tradition   71

CHAPTER   11 Boxes and chests   79

CHAPTER   12 Clocks   85

CHAPTER   13 From the Orient: Chinese and Asian art   90

CHAPTER   14 Antiquities and tribal art   99

CHAPTER   15 Samplers and beadwork   105

CHAPTER   16 Textiles, lace, costume and fashion   108

CHAPTER   17 Style and the new order; Art Nouveau   116

CHAPTER 18 Sculptures and the Belle Époque 119

CHAPTER 19 Art Deco 124

CHAPTER 20 Architectural and Garden antiques 126

CHAPTER 21 Kitchenalia and household 135

CHAPTER 22 Jewellery and items from the lady's boudoir 140

CHAPTER 23 Weapons- Warfare and hunting 145

CHAPTER 24 Miscellaneous and curiosities 151

CHAPTER 25 Ephemera, toys and games 156

CHAPTER 26 Coins and medals 162

Appendix I   A rough guide to values 166

Appendix II   Glossary of terms 169

Appendix III Care and repair of antiques 177

Appendix IV   Selected Flea markets 181

Appendix V   Common bartering terms 182

Appendix VI   French numbers and pronunciation 183

Index 184

INTRODUCTION

This book is not aimed at professional antiques dealers or collectors for whom money is no object; they can visit the many expensive-end antique shops and fairs in Paris, Le Mans and other major towns where they will find antiques of recognizable quality and prices to match. At such places items will have been through several dealers hands and so are no longer treasures but commodity stock, available to those who can afford high-end prices.

This book is about treasure hunting in France. That magical term 'treasure hunting' means different things to different people, but no matter how it is applied, it has a unique way of stirring the imagination. But the definition I like most about the word treasure is anything valued or preserved as precious in someone's eyes at some point in time. Hunting is the process of searching carefully for something, often unknown, until it is found and this is precisely what this book sets out to demonstrate.

For me treasure hunting is not a pursuit for wealth in the form of jewels or precious objects; nor is it the monetary value that is important but the unique quest to hunt down those 'sleeping' treasures on and under tables at French flea markets. The vast majority of treasures I have found over the years are of only modest monetary value, but every single one has a story to tell, each is a little gem in its own right and a true fragment of the past.

When I stumble upon what we call a sleeper, whether it is a 19thcentury candlestick or a 2,000 year old relic from Egypt or Rome, I like to reminisce I am holding in my hands something which belonged to a very different world to ours, made and used by people from a distant time and culture. In fact, people are what this book is really all about. I wonder where these things have been all those years, who has kept them safe, perhaps treasured them and how they ended up in a small rural flea market, perhaps thousands of years since their creation. Such finds often have the appearance of being stored away out of sight. Years, centuries even, of patination, dust and cobwebs testify to a life spent in a barn or attic, and only exposed to daylight in a bid to make a little money; items not wanted or appreciated; trifles, considered to be lacking any or precious little value.

All the illustrations are from my own collection built up over some thirty years. I have travelled the length and breadth of France and never cease to be amazed by the cultural differences between the areas. This is perhaps never better illustrated than by the ubiquitous café au lait bowl and simple country faïence pottery dish which are synonymous with the French way of life. They have signature styles of decoration which are unique to individual regions of France. But it has been in rural Normandy and its environs which have proved the most lucrative hunting ground. I think this is largely the result of its isolation, in part from tourism, unlike central and southern regions which have been exposed to the antique trade for far longer.

It is necessary to understand these regional differences as old traditions can continue largely unchanged down to the present day. It is also essential to acquire a basic knowledge of antiques and collectables in order to spot the genuine and old from the modern and reproduction. No single printed work can ever provide a tool which will teach the subtle differences in patina wear and design; only handling can fully achieve this skill and only by time will your eye mature to the extent that spotting antiques will become second nature. In the pages to come, I have tried to provide a taste of the possibilities of treasure hunting in French markets and the enjoyment which is very much part of the French flea market experience.

Fig. 1 Le Mans Flea market

If you have never experienced the French flea market then it is impossible to fully explain the air of excitement as you step out on a wonderful early morning, dark and crisp with a slight chill in the air. The sound of church bells ringing out to summon the righteous to prayer as though in competition with the frenzied activity taking place outside its portals. The noise levels begin to rise, slowly at first, with people effusively wishing one another the compliments of the day as they unpack their cars and vans, laying out their treasures ready to attract the eager buyer. So enjoy the experience of learning about antiques in this little guide and take that short ferry crossing and soak up the wonderful atmosphere that is the French flea market.

CHAPTER 1
Flea markets and Vide greniers

Thanks to the host of English television programms where teams travel to a French market to buy and later attempt to sell for a profit, has made visiting a flea market ever more popular with visitors to France. Every region holds them; in fact few towns are spared the closure of roads, a necessary local inconvenience in order to facilitate them. If you see the sign *ROUTE BARREE*, it often means a flea market is taking place nearby. Most events will be held on weekends, the majority on Sundays and invariably there will be some on a public holiday. For the French, the flea market and vide greniers are an enjoyable part of summer life and whilst the average French browser might not be the biggest of spenders, they arrive in vast numbers. It is often a family outing, enjoying the opportunity to wander in the fresh air, meet friends, and of course in true French style, enjoy a meal and a glass of wine or simply a croissant and coffee whilst watching the world go by.

There are numerous major flea markets in Paris, including the popular Porte de Vanves on the western side, but the most important flea market and probably the most famous in Europe is Marché aux Puces St-Ouen de Clignancourt, situated at Saint-Ouen on the northern fringe of Paris. Strictly speaking it isn't a single market but a grouping of more than a dozen flea markets which total more than two thousand stalls and shops which sprawl over six hectares of residential suburbs.

Here the treasure hunter can find an eclectic mix of vintage, country, Paris apartment, cottage, rustic chic and shabby styles, in fact, virtually everything from antiques to junk. Situated less than thirty minutes from the centre of Paris, it is the favoured haunt of serious antique buyers and the more intrepid collector. I am always in my element here, around so many things that are old but new to me.

As with all flea markets, it is important to arrive early while the morning is still young. It may be dark but it is at this point when the dealer is setting his table that the treasure hunt should begin. Some items might be old favourites, their fading price tickets testimony to countless days in the sun waiting for someone to snap them up, but others will be new to the table and their desirability as yet untested by the passing trade. I always think those following later will only see what others have seen and dismissed.

Generally speaking there are two kinds of sellers. There are those who use the art of display and lovingly curate their collection either in smart shops or outside on tables under brightly coloured canopies. Their presentation painstakingly put together suggesting they are not necessarily concerned whether or not you buy anything. In fact, you might get the impression that their display would be upset if you did take something away. But I can assure you they are very keen to relieve you of your money as they will always have something else to keep the presentation neat and tidy. Then there are those who don't care what their stall looks like, piling it high in a jumble, with little sense of arrangement or order. Others simply tip their stock onto blankets on the ground, but this does not imply incredibly low prices. Dealers often use this psychological ploy to make you think you have found something which the stallholder does not value just because it is on the floor, but beware; this is often not the case. The whole air of the Parisian flea market is very cosmopolitan and of course, there seems to be jazz on every corner which is invariably Django Reinhard, gipsy style.

Fig.2 Some stalls are neatly curated as here at a Paris flea market

The word flea market, French *marché aux puces*, originated sometime in the eighteenth century when chiffoniers, or rag-and-bone men, resold goods and clothing found in aristocrats' rubbish bins. The craze soon caught on and very quickly the poorer elements of society were bringing along flea-infested furniture and other household items, which they sold to the public. They set up their stalls here at the present day Porte de Clignancourt, just outside the gates of Paris, in order to avoid fees and taxes incurred within the city walls. Mind you, it's a disputed theory, and has been argued over by historians and linguists for more than half a century, but I think it's likely to be largely true.

In the south are two of my favourite weekend haunts, the Montpellier, which is really a brocante in that it is for professional sellers, and the Villeneuve-lès-Avignon flea market, both situated in the picturesque Provence region. Whilst once again prices can be quite high, there are still 'sleepers' hiding amongst the general stock.

Right across France there are tens of thousands of vide greniers (literally empty your attic) and braderies. These both equate to the English boot fair. One of the largest is the Braderie at Lille which boasts over 10,000 pitches and requires a considerable amount of energy to navigate the maze of streets and alleyways. However, on balance, I find the smaller 'once a year' venues much more rewarding as they are predominantly a mix of local dealers and the ordinary public who have cleared out their attic, garage or deceased relative's effects. Here, one can find treasures that have not been through the professional trade and might be seeing the light of day for the first time in decades. A particular favourite of mine is situated in the Orne department in north-western France, and possibly one of the most picturesque settings for such an event. The venue is a long 4 kilometre road which passes through woods, linking the communes of Bagnoles de l'orne and Saint-Michel-des-Andaines. Along this straight tree-lined forest road some three thousand stalls are set out with everything imaginable. Four o'clock in the morning is the hour when all serious buyers leap out of bed and into the darkness of night with torches primed and ready. The long road through the forest is an eerie place at this time of the morning. Figures, no more than fleeting silhouettes with flickering torches, make their way along the road. On both sides of this woodland thoroughfare, numbers and divisions have been chalked on the tarmac and thousands of cars and vans leisurely find their spot.

Fig. 3 Some dealers tip their goods on a sheet on the ground.

Some sellers slump behind their steering wheel and catch forty winks before setting up their stall. The hardier, seasoned dealer will welcome buyers hovering, waiting as he unloads his spoils. Early sales are eagerly sought as they prime the seller for the long day ahead. It is not unusual in the dark hours before sunrise, to stumble upon little groups of sellers sitting around a candle-lit table drinking wine, unhurried by the passing hunters with their torch beams falling on empty pitches, unconcerned that their stock for the day has not yet been laid out or scanned by eager buyers. Despite this, the treasure hunt always begins when the first car or van arrives. The 'early bird catches the worm' is never more appropriate than here. It is vital to be out while the morning is still fresh, even though dreary-eyed stallholders might be standing around dipping croissants in their black coffee in between tossing dour jokes across adjacent stalls.

They will be watching every passer-by, ready to spring into action if they think a sale might be imminent, or ripe for negotiation.

For me there are several parts to the hunt, each in its own way important. The first, of course, spotting the treasure before others, but not appearing to be too keen. Then the face- to- face psychology between buyer and seller begins. This is the point which will make or break a deal. The seller will quickly expound the merits of the piece, often adding snippets of made-up invention to 'gild the lily' in order to justify his opinion of its rarity or monetary value. At the same time the experienced buyer will act nonchalantly, looking for anything which might devalue the item, a chip, dent or patination which he will point out to the seller. I have even used the trick of putting the item back on the table to give the impression I am not that interested, unless of course, the price is right. But there is danger to this tactic, as another may snatch it from under your nose and secure the purchase, as I have done on occasion to others. A good and old friend of mine who is a serious buyer of French antiques and collectables and who endlessly trawls every fair he can find in France, virtually every day of the week, once said 'There is so much competition out there

Fig.4 Eclectic mix of antique and retro architectural collectables.

Fig. 5 Rural town fairs offer a unique ambience below the sound of the Church bells.

that every day is a fight, every week is a battle and every month is a war and the day I don't win, I shall retire.' There is often a comical side to the flea market. In most cases pitches are marked out with lines and numbers which delineate each space, some suitable for cars and others for vans.

Many serious dealers like to have their own spot and will book that for the day, so it is rarely a matter of choice when stallholders arrive. This invariably leads to total confusion with vehicles arriving from different directions all meeting up in the centre of town. The quietness is broken by yellow-jacketed stewards barking out orders as they wrestle with the chaos. Eventually, when everyone has found the designated spot to set up their stall, all is once again relatively calm. But even then the excitement can suddenly erupt when a steward brandishing his tape measure confronts a stallholder and tells him 'you are taking up fifty centimetres more space than you are allowed' or they might have set their table slightly over the line. The result is that tempers fly and the disgruntled seller has to lift his table to the correct spot.

Fig. 6 A dealer unloading his latest house clearance at Agon Coutainville.

More than once have I witnessed this spectacle when a folding table has opened mid-point and china and glass has smashed to the ground and the disgruntled seller has to lift his table to the correct spot. There is little or no formality to these fairs. The Mayor will usually be in attendance, and, it is not unusual to see this esteemed head of the community decked out in overalls and in the foray of the various tasks. When it comes to the local aristocracy who reside in the nearby chateau, they are extremely unlikely to make an appearance as there is no longer any tradition of 'noblesse oblige'.

You will often find both professional dealers and amateur householders side by side at these street markets. The former will have interesting and saleable items, but what fascinates me the most is what householders sell, or perhaps I should say, what they are unlikely to sell. It is not unusual to see a tea cup with its handle missing or something which is so corroded that it appears it is only the rust which is holding it together. And when it comes to woodworm, it is often expounded as a good sign, and testimony to its great age and rarity, although that is rarely the case. I think for many simple householders it is not so much the necessity to make money, but more the social aspect which makes them habitually turn out once a year. Typically from 6 am to 6 pm they will spend the whole long day in the sun, or pouring rain! What I love most is meeting these people and I can assure the reader that there are treasures to be found by those who are diligent, even if on occasions they might be few and far between.

Fig. 7 Rummaging through boxes for treasure, someone will find a little gem.

There are many similar types of events including Foire à Tout which is a fair of everything, Marche de Livres, book fair, Bourse aux Vétements, clothes and fabric fair and Bourse Militaire which specializes in military collectables. The salon des antiquites, a 'high end' sale of antiques by professionals, is usually held inside the local hall.

Most administrative towns will have a Salle de Vente which is an auction room offering catalogued sales of antiques, works of art, collectables etc.

For the serious buyer there is the vente aux enchères d'antiquités.
These are high-end auctions, mostly situated in larger towns. Beware, it is necessary to have a very good grasp of the French language, because bidding can be rapid and difficult to keep up with.

All over France there are dealers selling their stock from the comfortable venue of a shop. The brocante or antiquité will usually offer higher priced antiques and collectibles which have been purchased by the dealer from house clearances and auctions. The dealer will have paid rather more for his stock and will have to pay taxes and probably rent as well so real bargains will be difficult to find, but by no means impossible. Few dealers have an insight into every class of antique, so there will always be the opportunity to discover a 'sleeper'. The second type of shop, or more often warehouse, is the Dépôt-vente. These differ from the Brocantes as the stock on sale has been brought in by members of the public. A mutual price has been agreed with the Dépôt-vente and this service is paid by way of commission. Again, bargains can be found, but these places mostly take in household items. Also, most if not all have selected dealers who will see any interesting items before the public do.

People often ask 'how do I find local flea markets in France?' The first port of call should be one of the many yellow guides such as Calendrier Des Brocantes et Vide-Greniers. This guide book, updated every year, covers the whole of France in convenient area issues and can be bought in most bookshops, tabacs and bars or can be purchased on line. There are a number of French Antiques magazines that regularly list events and of course local newspapers will have some local forthcoming fairs.

If you are unable to visit France personally, the internet offers the chance to buy from those who do. Again, the same rules apply. No dealer knows everything and bargains can and have been made on internet sites by people with knowledge of specific items. Online shops offer some of the best French vintage antiques and collectables. Take a look at ebay.uk where there are thousands of sellers such as simply-chateau or café-de-paris. They provide a great insight as to what can be found and a general guide to values.

Fig. 8 Crowds as far as the eye can see at Lisieux early afternoon.

TOP TIP

Bartering is an integral part of buying at any fair or brocante in France. Most dealers will expect to be 'knocked down' over their prices, but there is no recognised bartering percentage, unlike England, where ten percent is usually acceptable. There are several phrases for ascertaining the lowest price 'Le petit prix' or 'le dernier prix' the last price but I prefer to use the phrase 'C'est combien?' – Literally, 'that is how much?' This is simply because you can later on ask for the last price. If you don't like the dealer's price, whatever you do, do not reply with 'C'est trop cher.' which means 'it's too expensive.' Firstly the dealer is likely to be offended, he will go to great lengths to explain why it is not expensive and the bartering will end abruptly. Far better is to say 'C'est trop cher pour moi'- 'it's too expensive for me.' This will in no way offend the dealer and invariably they will ask you what you would like to pay for it and the dialogue can continue. Also do not be lured into thinking, because a faded price label means an object has been for sale for some time, that it will be a potential bargain if bought at a 'knock down price.' Ask yourself why has it not been snapped up by the many buyers who will have seen it? Perhaps it is too expensive, in which case it might be worth making an offer. But more likely is that it is not what it appears to be; is it a reproduction or does it have damage which has been skilfully concealed? So the moral here is, buyer beware when it comes to faded labels.

CHAPTER 2

Lighting the home; Candlesticks and lanterns.

Fig. 9 Zoomorphic pricket candlestick

The candle is amongst man's oldest solutions to combat the loss of light at night, and although early candles produced limited close illumination, people's lives were restricted by the limits set by sunrise and sunset. Candles can be traced back to Roman times in Europe, but artificial lighting goes back tens of thousands of years. Prehistoric man invented the wax lamp and examples have been discovered in caves and subterranean flint mines. Of simple form, these early lamps were created by hollowing out rock chalk and laying a flax thread in fat, the light though meagre, allowed early mankind to work and paint in these dark places.

Although most prehistoric lamps were not portable and therefore will not be found, the same is certainly not true for candlesticks and lanterns which are amongst the most frequently seen objects at any flea market. However, the greatest majority will be of more recent age, often copying earlier types. The candlestick has evolved slowly over several thousand years, but the story of the French candle holder really begins in the Middle Ages when an earthen floored home would have had an iron spike hammered into the ground and a tallow candle pushed into the point. By the fourteenth century iron prickets had tripod feet as Figure 10 below, which is most likely a 17thcentury example. Also at this time we find evidence of the rushlight, a simple device consisting of a small bundle of rushes, 18 inches or so long which were dipped in used kitchen fat and inserted into an iron holder.

Few early iron candle and rushlight holders now survive and it is to the bronze or brass types which we will now focus. It was probably due to the indigenous deposits of calamine, the key ingredient of brass occurring in abundance in Belgium and France, which accounts for the early brazing and manufacture of candlesticks in the Low Countries. It has inevitably resulted in a higher abundance of survivals here in France.

Fig. 10 & 11   17th / 18th century iron pricket candlesticks with feet.   The left with spike, the right with candle holder.

The Gothic candlesticks in Figure 12 are good examples from the early 16th century. Made in brass, these are now rare and difficult to find and as a result, are in much demand from collectors. The treasure hunter can very occasionally find early pieces like these, but generally speaking, it is not until the seventeenth century that candlesticks become more common. The emergence of trade across the Low Countries and beyond resulted in candlesticks arriving from Holland in a new distinctive style. In many ways these new arrivals were bringing back the old tradition of pricket candlesticks. Figure 14 shows a pair of Dutch East Indies prickets from the late 17th century. By the 18th century well-to-do homes in France demanded candlesticks which were in keeping with the new order of style and decoration and this led to the octagonal stepped Louis XV type which is still reasonably common at flea markets. Unfortunately, they were often silver plated in imitation of fine silver and this devalues them as the silvering will be patchy, making them less desirable in that condition. The most commonly found candlesticks are the side ejector type, Figure 16; the earlier 18[th]century examples have attractive petal bases and octagonal lower stems. They slowly evolve into plain round bases during the 19th century.

Another frequently seen candleholder is the Rat de cave or cellar rat Figure 18 It was extensively used throughout France in wine cellars lighting the room and checking the fermenting gases which could be dangerous if the flame was extinguished. The typical example consists of a turned fruitwood base and spiral iron shaft which has an internal stump which can be lowered or raised, to control the height of the flame as the wick burns down. The handle or rat's tail is ideal for carrying the light and to hang it on the edge of an oak barrel. Other derivatives include birdcage candlesticks and the hogscraper.

Fig. 12 Gothic L.1500, R 1550 .

Fig. 13 17[th]century

Fig.14 Dutch East Indies around 1660.

Fig. 15. Louis XV 1720   Fig.16 18th19thcent. ejector   Fig.17. Rococo Boulle

Chamber sticks or pans form another group. Early examples are often of the walled-pan form and made in repousse' sheet brass. These were essentially utilitarian and as such were not often subjected to the dictates of fashion. They were not intended to be static like candlesticks, but designed to be carried around the house, and in particular, taking the dark route to the bed chamber.

Fig. 18 Rat de cave 19thcentury    Fig. 19 Tin Hogscraper candlestick 19thc.

An old word for lantern was 'lanthorn' a reference to the horn that once formed the panes. Glass was expensive and easily broken whereas horn was tough and long lasting, and although it was yellow and not clear like glass, it allowed enough light through to provide illumination. These often have conical roofs with ventilation holes to let the air in and heat out, along with a hinged door. When a light was needed outside, candles were used in these lanterns. Fig. 21.

At the turn of the twentieth century, there were more brass candlesticks in France than I believe anywhere else in Europe. When electricity arrived, people in rural France did not go out and buy electric lamps, instead, they converted candlesticks into lamps in vast quantities. Having said this, most were converted by travelling tinkers whose skills varied greatly. Some sticks were neatly fitted with quality conversion elements, others poorly done. Unfortunately many a fine candlestick has had a hole drilled through the side of the base for the electric cable and thereby these are of little value now.

Fig. 20 17th century wrought iron fat lamp.

Fig. 21 Iron lantern, originally with horn windows 1880s.

Fig.22 Carved wood Church altar pricket candlestick. Around 1700.

Fig. 23. Faience pottery chamber stick Around 1900.

TOP TIP

Dating candlesticks can be difficult as early styles have long been reproduced but one thing usually distinguishes an antique candlestick from a modern reproduction and that is the base. Turn the candlestick upside down and if the underside of the base is smooth and beautifully finished, then it is likely to be old. Whereas if it is roughly finished it will most certainly be modern. You see, a period craftsman would pay as much attention to the underside as to the rest: it was his pride, unlike modern copyists.

Fig. 24   Antique. Smoothly finished and reproduction. Rough casting

If the candlestick has an ejector hole, this will show signs of use where a sharp point has been inserted to remove a candle stump. It is important to be familiar with the look and feel of old brass as it should have acquired a patina, a very smooth soft surface. However, even a reproduction of the late 19th early 20th century may well have acquired some patina and wear through prolonged use, so patina alone is not enough to date a piece. The only way to determine whether a piece of brass is antique is by considering its style, weight, colour, wear, construction and surface patina. Only then can you make an accurate decision. The figure 25 below shows what appears to be a 17th century pricket candlestick of Gothic form. Candlesticks of this period would not be composed of separate parts like this.   This is clearly a late 19th century copy. True, it has acquired a convincing patina, but has a tell-tale machine-made   screw running down its entire length.

Fig. 25 Gothic- style brass candlestick and component parts

CHAPTER 3

Pewter

The French have had a particularly long association with pewter. It was still widely used right up until the nineteen sixties and even today, despite the potentially dangerous lead content, it is still used by the odd farmworker in rural areas. Early examples are exceptionally rare and none more so than the 14th century octagonal flagon in Figure 26. I discovered it in a box of oddments a few years ago at a small flea market and purchased it for just one euro! It turned out to be worth much more. I think it demonstrates how here in rural France, museum pieces like this can still be found by the diligent treasure hunter. In 1701 Louis XIV made an ordinance which ordered his subjects to give away their silver for coining, to help pay for the recent wars. This single act served to provide the pewterers with a sudden and substantial demand for their products which resulted in a golden age for pewter.

Fig. 26. Rare 14th century octagonal French flagon

Along with the more traditional pewter forms, they now made pieces to replace the melted-down silver, and silver forms were suddenly widely made in pewter. The wine measure has been an important part of French life for over two hundred years. The true measure arrives in around 1790 after the great French statesman Talleyrand pushed the academy to adopt an accurate model for weights and measures. This was achieved by standardizing the weight and capacity of these vessels into metric units of kilos and litres. They often bear verification marks, most commonly on the lid or handle. Our Figure 27 has distinctive acorn thumb piece, which is the standard for most Normandy types. Mustards, the early examples in rococo style, can still be found as well as 18th century salts with spiral fluting form. Porringers, two-handled porridge and liquefied food bowls, Figure 30, can also be early, although the majority seen will be later copies.

Fig.27 Normandy flagon   Fig 28 Tankard dated 1767   Fig. 29. 19th century measure.

Fig.30 Porringer late 18th century.

Detail of owners stamp on handle. Note the inverted S.   Fig. 31 Mustard pot 18th c.

Figure 32 Salt. German c.1750   Figure 33 Italian architectural salt. 18th c.

During the Middle Ages and up until the middle of the 20th century, food was often served on pottery or pewter plates. However, in the early period the poorer elements of society would have used wood or pottery bowls and platters; only the middle to upper classes could afford pewter. But by the nineteenth century when industrial processes made pewter more readily available and thus affordable, most households used pewter for everyday use so vast quantities of 19th century pewter survives in France. The plate and bowl were the principal utilitarian items during the 17th and 18th century. At this period they were often very plain or at best, with single- reeded edges. Wriggle- work was fashionable mainly in England and Holland between 1660 and 1740 and usually comprises animals, birds and flowers in imitation of late 17th-century delftware. Occasionally one comes across marriage plates. Our example in Figure 35 uses birds to symbolize the union of husband and wife. Above, a flaming sun denoting happiness and the cross to show the union is in the eyes of the Lord.

 Possibly one of the most common French household utensils was the chamber pot, thousands were made but few survive today. This is probably because their usefulness did not outlast the 19th century, or at least not in any great quantity. They had more value for their metal content and the itinerant workers who turned candles into lamps, bought them for scrap value. The pewter candlestick was also a very common household item, but due to the rough nature of removing candle stumps and rough-handling on a soft metal, few early examples survive, and those that do are often battered.

Fig.34. 17th century broad –rim charger.

Fig. 35. Wrigglework marriage plate around 1700.

TOP TIP.

Old pewter has a wonderful sensuous silvery patina which is difficult to reproduce although, despite this, even copies made half a century or so ago may, by now, have acquired some dulling oxides. Fakes are not common, they can be distinguished from reproductions by the simple fact that they were made to deceive. Reproductions on the other hand were made in the antique style. Fakes usually have a man-made corrosion which resembles a regular speckling, something you would never find in natural processes and they are occasionally even deliberately battered and dirty under a layer of grease. Reproductions tend to have a stiff-looking, often clumsy appearance, but even examples made in the early 20th century, are likely to have acquired some wear and patination. Touchmarks can be helpful in dating pewter but, like so many other things, they were copiously copied, sometimes to create a fake, but more often they are merely modern representations of old marks. Knowledge of the types of touchmarks and the correct places of marking will help to weed out the genuine from the fake. Finally, pieces with 17thcentury dates should be viewed with caution, if a piece looks too good to be true, then it probably is!

Fig.36 Broad-rim bowl 1680-1700

Fig.37 18thc. candlestick

Fig. 38 Typical pewter touchmarks, pseudo silver hallmarks, engraved lids with dates. 1750s-20th century.

CHAPTER 4

Silver and white metal

It was not until around the 1650s that food was consumed using metal implements. Up until then food was generally eaten with the fingers on wooden or pottery platters. By the close of the seventeenth century the French had developed a system of laying a formal table using pewter, brass, porcelain or silver cutlery and other European countries quickly followed this new method of dining. Early pieces of this date are now hard to find following the mass melting of silver ordered by Louis XIV in 1701. This had been ordered so as to replenish the French royal treasury, which had been depleted by years of war. This nation-wide action robbed the country of most of its fine early silver.

Arguably the most important period in French silver was during the reign of Louis XV between 1735 and 1750 when silver cutlery became more decorative. This was the beginning of the Rococo style with its distinctive sinuously curving forms along with shell and scroll motifs, a decorative elegance which impacted on the rest of Europe. It is unlikely that many pieces will be found today outside exclusive antique shops and anything resembling this style will probably be a revival piece from the second Rococo style which popularized French silver from the 1830's until the close of 19th century. By the 19th century, master silversmiths were producing ever extravagant pieces, invariably in line with prevailing ornamental trends and not only in Paris, but also in the large cities. Despite the comparative rarity of master silversmiths work, there are still sleepers to be found. The fine coffee pot on Figure 39 was bought at a small flea market for less than 5 euros. Close inspection revealed the distinctive french poincon (hallmark) for French silver, the head of Minerva stamped on each separately cast section of the pot. But what made this piece even more significant was the mark of Froment Meurice a Parisian silversmith of distinction.

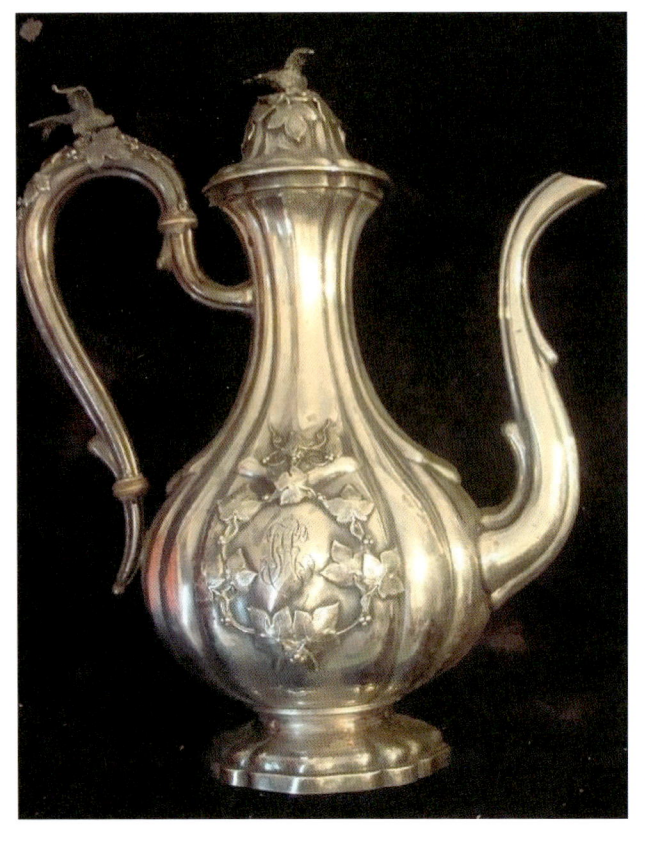

It is not unusual to come across examples of English silver with the familiar set of hallmarks, particularly Georgian tankards and salts of which I have found numerous examples over the years. The silver fox stirrup cup in Figure 42 is a good example. The Georgian hallmarks were all but lost amongst the hair detail and clearly missed by the seller who stated it was pewter! It is true to say that many dealers and householders are not familiar with English hallmarks.

.Fig.39 Coffee pot by Froment Meurice 1880 sold for £600

This is perhaps made more difficult because the marking positions are completely different from french metalwork.

I am not quite certain how honest some French sellers are. The common statement thrown at you when you pick up a piece of what looks like silver is 'C'est argent massif.' Take it from me, it rarely is solid silver, instead it will more likely be no more than silver plate.

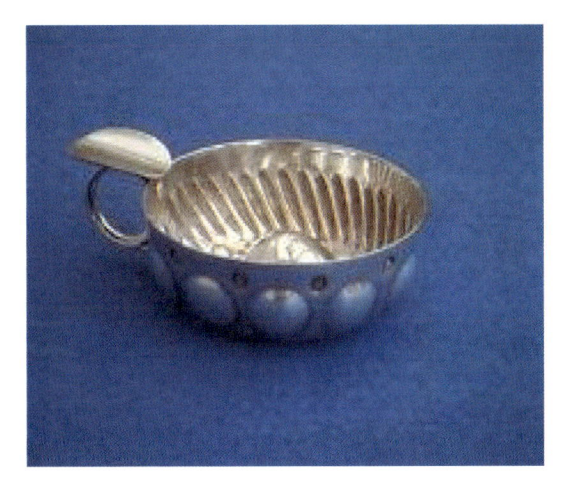

Fig 40. Taste de vin- wine taster

Fig41 Ornate French bob-bon dish.

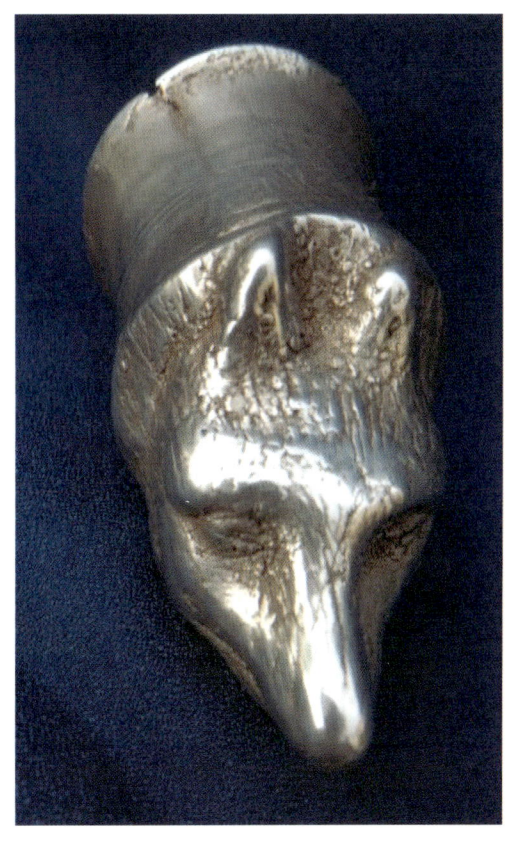

Fig.42. Silver fox stirrup cup around 1800.

A couple of years ago the International price of silver went through the roof. This had the effect of transferring the value of many pieces to the melting pot and raising the expectations of dealers and sellers alike. Even today, when the silver melt value has dropped to its earlier level, the remaining pieces for sale often still retain that high value melt component in the price.

Fig. 43. 18th-19th century silver cutlery

Fig.44 Serving utensils

Silver & gilt 1900

Fig.45 Detail with typical grotesque head.

TOP TIP

English hallmarks always have a lion passant and have the great advantage of date letters which gives a very precise year of manufacture, Figure 46. French silver cannot be dated accurately in the same way. In France there has been a vast usage of different marks, from various male heads to Cockerel's, animal parts and hundreds of town marks. The most common poincon, as they are known, consists of the head of Minerva and the makers mark in a lozenge. This mark was used from 1838 and right through the 20th century, so it can be seen from this, that style and ornament are often the only accurate means by which to date a piece of French silver.

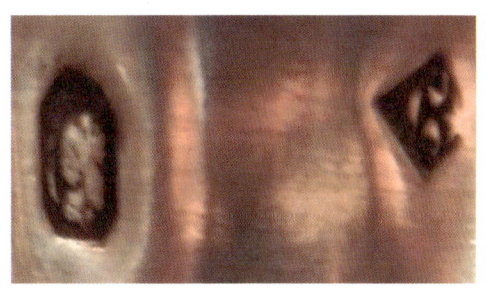

Fig.46 English hallmark with makers initials Elkingtons & Co, anchor for Birmingham, lion passant for sterling silver and date letter C for 1902

Fig.47 French poincon- head of Minerva. Makers mark in a lozenge. Around 1870.

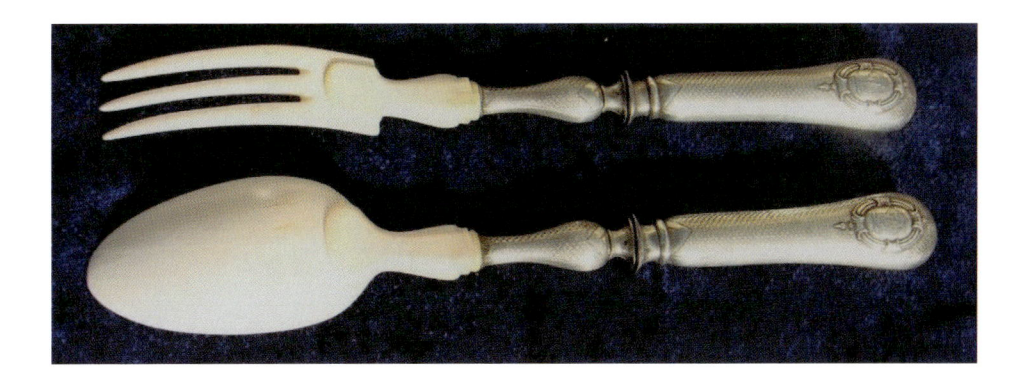

Fig. 48. Salad servers with ivory bowl and tines

Silver plate.

Plated silver does not necessarily equate to a lesser quality item than solid silver. In France there are several names synonymous with quality, but by far the most famous is that of Christofle. The Paris firm of Christofle was founded in 1830, when Charles Christofle took control of the jewellery workshop belonging to his wife's family. In 1842 Charles made a strategic leap forward when he secured electroplating rights from the English silversmiths of Elkingtons of Birmingham. Within a few years he had become an industrial leader producing silver picture frames, comports, dishes, bowls and a huge variety of mainly dinner accessories. He was quick to adopt the changing styles of each emerging period. Japonesque, Art Nouveau and rococo revival, the latter being their most prolific and longest lasting style. Before the close of the 19th century, the firm had invented Gallia ware, a metal similar to pewter, but looking more like silver. Marks changed over the years but the principal ones to look out for are the pair of scales and the later Cockerel with Gallia metal below.

Fig. 49 Dish with dolphins by Christofle 1900

CHAPTER 5

Delft and Faïence pottery

In 16th century Europe, the main focus for faience production was Italian maiolica, but comparatively little seems to have survived compared to later faïence, as a result it is extremely rare and hard to find. By the early 17th century, the centre of gravity for tin-glazed production had shifted north of the Alps. The most significant production of tin-glazed pottery began in the Netherlands, principally from 1615-1740. The earliest pieces marked a new process which involved glazing pots entirely in a white tin glaze instead of covering only the painted surface. These early potters soon began applying a clear glaze which gave great depth to the cobalt blue decoration, thought to be in imitation of Chinese porcelain. By 1640 the Delft potters were directly copying Chinese designs, taking advantage of a shortfall of porcelain coming out of China at this time. The Dutch seized the opportunity by exporting large quantities of tin-glazed ware, in Chinese taste, to Europe. The Dutch East India Company was the main exporter and its products were characterized by Kraak-style wares, Figure 50, which within a decade, had flooded the market right across Europe. . These tin-glazed Kraak-style chargers, so called because the Portuguese had earlier exported Chinese porcelain in ships called carracks, directly copied Chinese Ming dynasty originals. The most noticeable design element is the paneling of decoration around the wide rim with copies of Oriental precious motifs.

Fig.50. Dutch Delft charger around 1670

Fig. 51. Delft fruit charger. C 1700

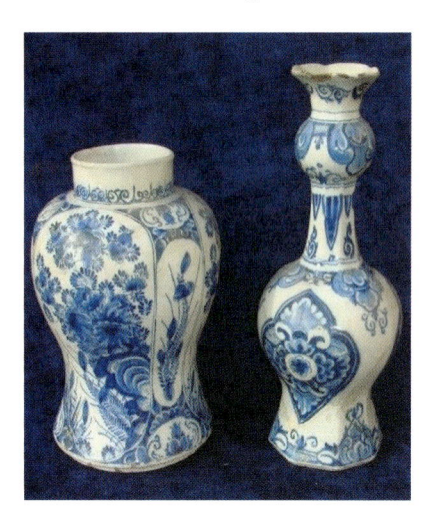

Fig. 52 Delft vases around 1800

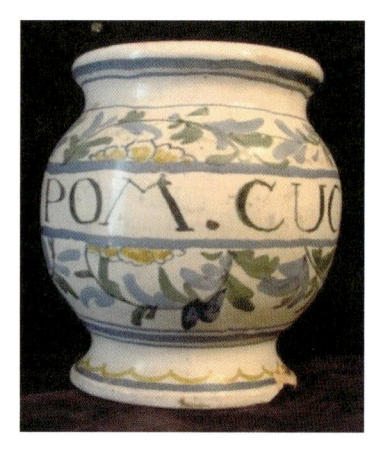

Fig. 53 French tin glaze drug jars 18th/19th century

Fig. 54 17th & 18th century tin glazed chargers, right hand dated 1713

Other popular themes of decoration were fruit, Figure 51, baskets of flowers, blue-dash tulip and portrait chargers, which are occasionally dated.

By 1700 factories in Holland, Germany and England were using enamel colours over the tin-glaze producing polychrome wares of great beauty, a medium which lent itself well to large commemorative chargers rather than just domestic table wares, as in Figure 54.

It is not until the middle of the 18th century that French potters began painting in hard-fired colours on unfired glazes, the earlier pieces often having brown-glazed backs. The principal pottery centres were at Rouen, Moustiers and Nevers, and these along with hundreds of smaller potteries throughout France, produced fashionable designs well into the 19th century

The production of faience had a considerable boost after Louis XIV silver melting edict. The result was a surge in demand for tableware in non-precious metals like faience. Of course the poorer classes had never processed silver, but with cheaper and more readily available pottery, they were now able to replace pewter and wooden utensils with this new tableware.

Fig. 55 Polychrome vase with heads 1780   Fig.56 Rouen faience water fountain 1800

The highly distinctive folk art pottery known as Quimper does not refer to simply one factory or maker producing faience wares, but the term is really generic of the French town where this particular style of hand-made pottery

Fig. 57 French faience 18th 19th century

was made, and by numerous potters.

This colourful Breton pottery is recognizable by its hand decorated designs reflecting the culture of this particular region of France and in particular the peasant designs, Figure 59, which began in the 1860s and the slightly later cockerel plates both of which are still quite plentiful.

In the Lorraine region we find an abundance of brightly-coloured wares associated with display china. The nearby Desvres pottery is known for its creamy white background decorated with bright blue, brilliant chrome yellow, iron red and sage green.

Fig.58 Desvres polychrome goat. 19th century

There are far too many centres of production than can be covered in this book, but other important potteries were operating at Luneville, Niederviller and Sarreguemines. In the Alsace, famous for its cooking pottery with floral decoration, the tradition is still very much alive, but beware, as it can be very difficult to distinguish the old from new.

Local faience is always pleasing to find and is generally in more abundance in southwest Burgundy, Beaujolais and the Loire region. The blue-rimmed, red-highlighted crockery is known in the area simply as Charolles, after the town. Although this rustic pottery is now just a sideline product, it is the main target of tourists wanting something reminiscent of the region to take home with them and has been for generations.

Fig.59 Quimper pottery

43

Fig. 60 Hand-painted

Fig. 61. Mark of Henriot, Quimper 1890s

Figure 62 Moulded in high relief.

Fig.63 Cockerel plate around 1880

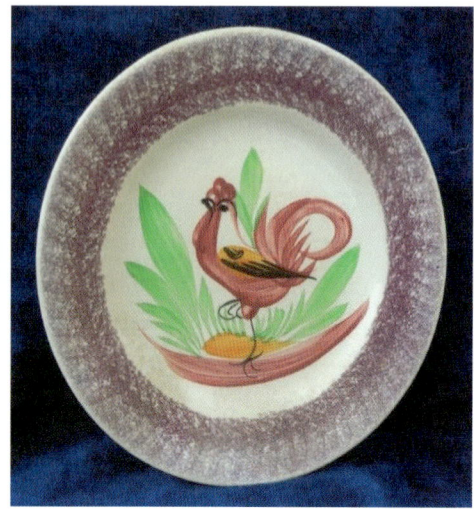

Fig. 64 Sponge- ware. 20th century

Fig.65. Tin-glaze slip-ware charger

Fig.66 Westerwald tankard 1700

Fig.67 Majolica conservatory seat around 1880

Fig.68 Luneville porcelain

TOP TIP

How can you possibly recognize antique from reproduction? Well, there is no easy way, but it pays to always be sceptical of any piece.

Feel the weight, copies are sometimes unreasonably heavy; consider the potting medium, is it porcelain, in which case it will be light, and is the decoration crisp and the colours bright. Tin-glazed earthenware will almost always show signs of its core material; if it does not, then be suspicious as flaking of the glaze is practically inevitable if the item has been used. The colour of the glaze should help determine where it was made. Generally speaking, Dutch Delft will have a hard white glaze and the body will have a reddish-buff colour, whereas English tin-glazed wares will have a bluish or pinkish white glaze and buff body. French faience tends to have reddish to buff body and green or blue tinted glaze. There are so many variables when it comes to faience, not least geographical, that generalizations can, at best, be a beginner's guide.

Fig.69 Typical glaze chips on French faience

Fig.70 Green/orange glaze on 17th century Rouen pottery

Fig. 71 17th century Hand-painted.

Fig.72 18th century hand-painted

Many pieces will bear factory or potters marks, mostly hand-painted rather than impressed, but whilst most will be authentic, copies of some of the more distinguished examples do exist.

Fig. 72 Transfer printing

Fig.73 Dutch Delft- maker Willem Kleftijus 1663

Fig. 74 French faience. 1760s

Fig, 75 Printed mark on porcelain

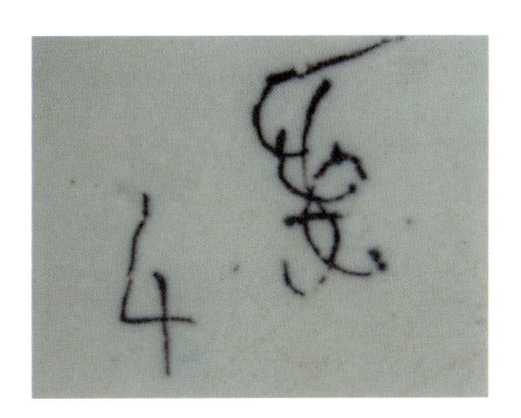

Fig. 76 Rouen Faience

Fig. 77 Paris drug jar 19th century porcelain

47

CHAPTER 6

Glass

The earliest glass vessels that can be dated are from ancient Egypt and more than 3,000 years old but the discovery of fragments found in western Asia suggests that the origins of glassmaking goes back to Mesopotamia around 2,000 BC.

Whilst it is still possible to find a piece of Egyptian or Roman glass, generally speaking glass vessels made before the eighteenth century are rare. The exception is perhaps bottles. Dark green glass wine bottles dating from the 17th-19th century can still occasionally turn up. The earliest are known as shaft and globe which is descriptive of their shape. Made from the 1630s, they are distinctive by their squat ogee body with tall tapering neck and wide string rim and basal kick. Early bottles like this and the later so-called onion bottle, often have extensive rainbow iridescence, testimony from centuries buried in the ground. Examples which have a moulded neck seal, bearing owners initials and date, are especially sought after and command very high prices. It is not until the 19th century that France begins to make a significant impact on ornamental glass manufacture. The true masters of French glass were Emile Galle, Lalique and the Nancy firm of Daum. Galle produced striking carved and etched cameo glass whilst Daum is characterized by its mottled multicoloured skin, acid-etched with botanical subjects. Lalique on the other hand developed the opalescent clear-glass vessels moulded in relief with female figures, birds and fish. Pieces such as these are unlikely to be encountered at a flea market, although Czechoslovakian copies are plentiful.

Fig. 78 Opalescent glass bowl with cherries

A fairly common example is the post 1920s glass bowl in a milky opalescence with three groups of cherries moulded on the round base and forming the tripod. Moulded mark is for G. Vallon, France. Figure 78.

Fig.79 18th & 19th century wine glasses    Fig. 80 Mercury candlestick

Mercury glass is a French product which was blown with silver mercury between layers to imitate silver. It was first produced in the 1850s and re-emerged in the early 20th century. By far the most common recipients for mercury glass were candlesticks like the example shown in Figure 80, but beware for although genuine antique examples are often seen, for every genuine one there might be five or six modern reproductions. The French national drink is wine and wine glasses have been produced in vast numbers for well over two hundred years. 18th century drinking glasses can still be occasionally found especially the heavy chunky ones made for the common man Figure 79, these are not easily broken and so survive in relatively large numbers. In contrast, the finely made examples, especially those which have been engraved, were very fragile and today are highly sought after and therefore expensive.

Fig.81 19/20th century pharmacy drug jars.

Fig.82 Heavy crystal tankard

Fig. 83 Wine bottle 1800   Fig.84. Mid 1800s

Blue glass drug jars were made in vast quantities for use in pharmacies all over France. Today, examples are plentiful and the range of labelling in Latin gives an interesting insight into early medicinal compounds.

Figs 85-87 examples of high-relief enameling.

Fig. 88 Engraved Art Nouveau decanter

Fig. 89 Glass biscuit barrel with ormolu mounts.

Top Tip

When considering whether a glass vessel is antique or modern, I turn it over and look carefully at the base. Where the external base of the glass would have made contact with a surface whether it be a table or stone sink, there will be a noticeable network of scratches, in fact the glass at this point is likely to be quite matt. A reproduction might also have scratches but these will generally run in the same direction, something which could never happen with a genuine antique piece. So the moral here is, if a piece of glass has no scratches on its base, it has not been used in a characteristic way and so can be presumed to be modern. If it has a good network of scratches which run in random directions, it is likely to have been used in a domestic setting and therefore will have some age.

CHAPTER 7

Mediaeval and later woodcarvings.

Figure 90. 14th century panel   Figure 91 Renaissance panel 1600

    Despite the fact that wood carving has always been widely practised, its survival is far less prevalent than most other common materials, being vulnerable to decay, insect damage and fire, but despite this, early and interesting examples can still be discovered in rural France.

Wood carving is a testimony to all those craftsmen who expressed themselves in every aspect of everyday life from religious beliefs to historical stories. From work, play and inventiveness to ancient tradition, handed down from distant ancestors. Some content will be entirely from the imagination of the woodworker whilst others will be influenced by ecclesiastical carving or book illustrations. Most early examples, and by that we mean pieces from the 14th-16th century, will be fragments from chests, or to be more precise, the panels from coffers and chests which were usually separately carved elements. The panel in Figure 90 is a typical 14th century example with its Gothic arcading, much like church windows of the period. The later Renaissance panel in Figure 91 is clearly French although it owes much to the woodcarvers of Italy. Whilst it's Italian inspired, Renaissance arabesque foliate scrolls are impressive, it is the central motif which is most notable element.

Fig. 92 carved wood cherub around 1600

Fig. 93 carved wood terms.

Fig. 94 carved wood & polychrome around 1700

Fig. 95 Polychrome cherub late 1800s

The central shield has the three dolphins, representing the French dauphin which is emblematic of the eldest son of the king of France (title in use from 1349-1830. Originally the title was solely granted to the Dauphin of Viennois, whose province in the French Alps came to be known as *Dauphiné*. Three dolphins were on the coats of arms of the Lords of Viennois. Up until the first quarter of the nineteenth century, the title was perpetuated by the eldest son of the king and the use of the three dolphins was used solely on his arms. It seems this panel has Royal connections and must have originated in a very grand and important piece of furniture. One wonders how it ended up in rural Normandy!

France was the key leader of the medieval Romanesque and Gothic movements and some of the finest examples can be seen in her great Cathedrals which are scattered in large numbers throughout the country. A century later the Renaissance impacted heavily upon French sculpture. Originating in Italy, the emerging movement became a blending of Italian art with French national style. These new classical forms were a breath of fresh air after the tired Gothic style and with the help from Italian sculptors who moved to France at this time, the movement rapidly took hold. The end of the feudal castle and the emergence of the chateau and new fun-loving aristocracy led to style. Renaissance sculpture is characterised by lightness and grace using decorative elements such as putti, satyrs, griffins and dolphins intermixed with a profusion of fruit and flowers, ribbons and scroll work.

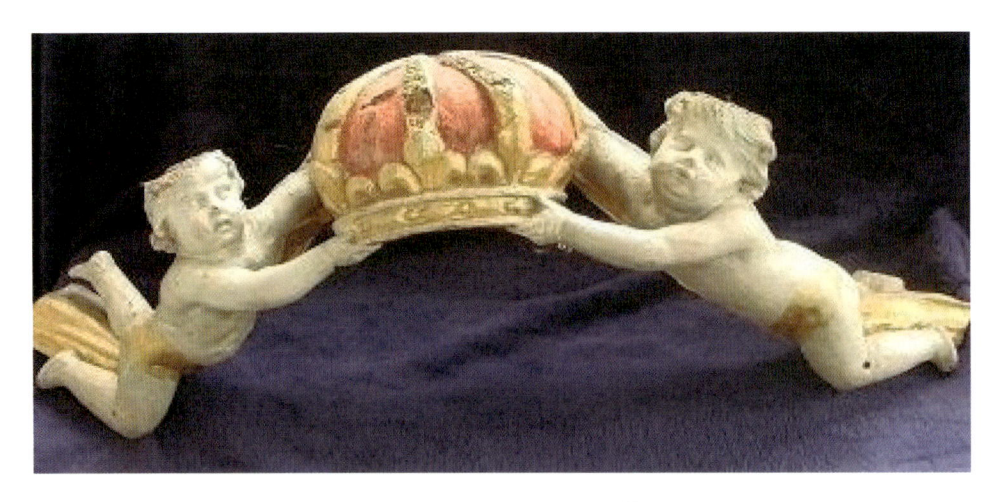

Fig. 96 Carved wood cherubs holding Royal crown

Most wood carvings found today, originated as components of French furniture. A frequently found class of wood carving is the cherub head or more accurately putti. The word originates from the Italian Putto meaning 'boy'. Most Renaissance putti are essentially decorative and are secular, representing a non-religious passion; a putto's presence symbolizes love, either Divine or of a more earthly nature. The putti holding the crown in Figure 96 is sending a different message. Removed from a chateau in the Orne region after a disastrous fire, it originally hung high above the entrance vestibule as a statement declaring allegiance to the king.

Fig. 97 Rare Romayne panel 1530 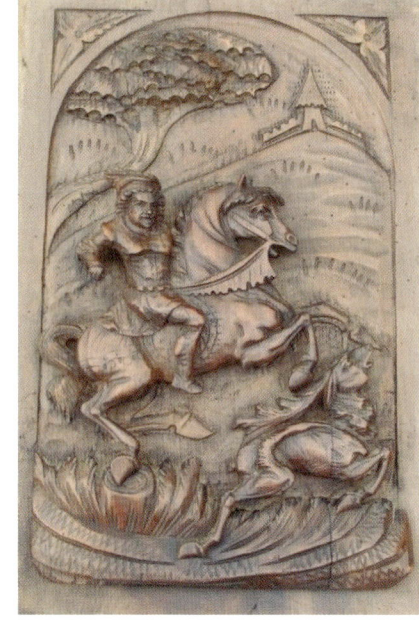   Fig. 98 Hunting scene panel 1880s

Top Tip

The art of carving wood goes back to the very earliest times, but giving a date to any piece requires two points of study. Wherever wood has been plentiful, mankind has used timber for housebuilding, the carver has had scope to show off his skills employing faux columns or pilasters, corbels and carvings. Inside, panels lining the walls or on furniture reflect the trends of the day, ranging from 15th century Gothic tracery to 16th century linenfold. Occasionally found are 16th and 17th century Romayne panels with human heads and later on, the various revivals of the 18th and 19th century. The problem is, all these decorative styles have been copied, and still are today. Patina and wear are the second consideration when attempting to date such pieces, but fakers often produce carvings which are flattened to suggest wear and having a high patina. So how do we separate these from the genuine? It all comes down to common sense. The faker will often grind the entire panel down to a consistent degree of wear, something which does not happen in the same way on a piece of wood which has formed part of something else. It might have 'fielded' edges, those extremities which were let into rebated stiles; these will not have been polished and neither will the back which should be lighter and free from all those years of polish and patina. Polishing removes raised detail leaving rounded edges to the upper parts of the carving. The lower detail will invariably survive in the same condition as it was originally carved.

Fig. 99 Conjoined cherubs 1700s.

CHAPTER 8

The Church and objects of devotion

Fig. 100 Carved wood and gilded dove of peace around 1600

Architectural pieces from French churches are fortunately quite rare in the market place. I say fortunately, because in an ideal world they would be revered for their historical importance. A few years ago at a rural flea market, I spotted a stall on which were heaped a number of very obviously early ecclesiastical pieces and all were for sale at very modest prices. After purchasing virtually all the early and exciting fragments, I learned the vendor was a retired cabinet maker who had been employed after the Second World War to repair damaged Churches. The pieces he was selling were basically fragments, often ravaged by woodworm or needing to be replaced for other reasons. The fact that some pieces were of 14th century date, did not seem of importance. Although I felt a tinge of conscience, I knew that if I didn't buy them, someone else would and most likely sell them without any regard for their historical merit. There is no doubting that 15th century linenfold panelling is rare and the example in Figure 102 would be difficult to find anywhere else in Europe. Stained glass is more abundant. The examples in Figures 106 & 107 are again from a Church, but sadly we may never know where they came from. Figure 106 depicts the miser, and might well be 16th/17th century, whereas Figure 107 is mid-19th century.

The Aumbry in Figure 101 is another fascinating relic from the Catholic Church. In its simplest form it is a cupboard or secure receptacle which was inserted deep in the side wall of the sanctuary or sacristy. Aumbries have been traditionally used to keep sacred vessels, books, reliquaries, and oils for anointing. Aumbries may also be used for the reservation of the Blessed Sacrament to store chalices and other vessels, as well as for the reserved sacrament, the consecrated elements from the Eucharist.

Fig.101 Aumbry cupboard   Fig. 102 15th century oak linenfold

Fig.103 14th century work

Fig. 104 Baptism chrémeau 1607

Fig. 105 Church bracket 1780

The dove in Figure 100 is carved from a single piece of wood and still has its original gold leaf finish. It originally hung above a pulpit where it represented the Holy Spirit as the dove of peace.

Church candlesticks and candelabra are surprisingly common objects at a flea market, especially country ones. I have a wrought iron five spiked pricket holder from around 1700 Figure 108 and the elaborate wood and plaster Gothic tower from around 1880. (Figure 110.)

Another interesting piece of Church equipment is the rectangular pewter casket Figure 104 with its hinged lid. It contains two small covered containers which held the holy oils necessary for the sacraments of baptism, confirmation and ordination. These small vessels are often referred to as "chrémeau" whose origin comes from the chrism, which is oil mixed with balm. Each oil is indicated by the initials of its Latin name engraved on the front of the casket: OS *(oleum catechumenorum)* for the oil of catechumens, SCH *(Sanctus chrisma)* for the chrism. It has the date 1607.

Objects of devotion in the home are far more numerous than those intended for ecclesiastical use. It has long been a tradition of Catholic families to hang crucifixes throughout their homes, or sometimes embedded into the foundation of the house. In the past most Catholics homes had a crucifix, secured to the wall or free-standing, positioned close to the main door that was used for entering and exiting the house, sometimes with a holy water font for making the sign of the Cross. Over the past couple of decades these have been taken down and are now one of the most often seen religious objects at any flea market. The Christian cross is a representation of the instrument of the crucifixion of Jesus and is the best-known symbol of Christianity

The cross is often shown in different shapes and sizes and in many different styles. It may be used in personal jewellery, or in domestic buildings. It is shown both empty and in crucifix form, that is, with a Figure of Christ, often referred to as the corpus (Latin for body), affixed to it. Most crosses are of the Latin type, in which the transverse beam is usually set two-thirds of the way up. They can be widely found in a multitude of different materials from wood to silver, brass, rock crystal and precious stones to those made simply from shell cases during the first World war.

Fig. 106 The miser 17th century glass panel. colours slightly muted.

Fig. 107 19th century stained glass earthy with vibrant, clear colours.

Fig.108 Candleholder 1600s

Fig. 109 Ormolu holy water stoop

Fig. 110 wood candle stand.

61

The history of icons and of their use in the Orthodox Church goes back many centuries. They were not a mere artistic device but were used as representations for instruction and as aids to piety, a window into heaven whereby a believer can meditate on the person whose portrait is on the icon. In this way an icon plays a role in enhancing the spiritual life of a believer.

Icons come in many forms; they may be painted on wood, embroidered on cloth, cast in metal, carved in stone, even printed on paper or metal. At first sight an icon might be thought to be artistic, but in fact nothing could be further from the truth There is very little room for artistic license. Almost everything within the image has a symbolic aspect. Christ, the saints, and the angels all have halos. Angels have wings because they are messengers. Figures have consistent facial appearances, hold attributes personal to them, and use a few conventional poses. Colour plays an important role as well. Gold represents the radiance of Heaven; red, divine life. Blue is the colour of human life etc. Letters are symbols too. Most icons incorporate some calligraphic text naming the person or event depicted. Even this is often presented in a stylized manner.

Fig. 111 Humble home Icon   Fig.112 Holy water stoop   Fig.113 Alabaster

Another, once common devotional device is the statue of Mary or one of the many Saints. Christianity arose from Judaism, which firmly rejected figurative religious art as being too much like idol worship, but once Christianity became the official religion of the Roman Empire in the 4th century, it was not long before Roman practices of portraying and honouring the divine would make their way into Christian practices as well.

Although Mary and the saints are portrayed in statue they are not worshipped as God is. Rather, the saints are venerated, meaning they are simply honoured and respected.

Statues come in many forms and made in countless materials from carved wood and stone to cast metal and plaster. In the home they promoted religious motivation and were often placed in niches built to receive them or even in miniature chapels. Domestic statues, unlike Church examples, never have crowns or any added accessories. Statues can still be occasionally glimpsed residing in exterior niches set into the front of buildings, but many more have been destined to the flea market.

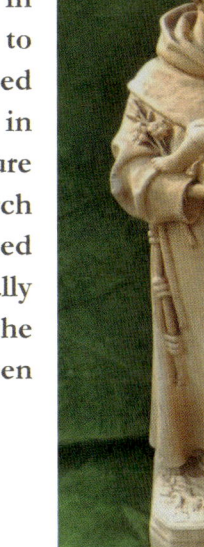

Fig.114 St. Anthony plaster figure

Fig. 115 1700s carved missal covers

Fig.116 Carved wood misericord-1650s

Fig.117 16th century reliquary casket.

63

CHAPTER 9

Mediaeval manuscripts and paintings

The oldest document I have come across dates from 1433 Fig.118 and is just one of many I have had the privilege to own. As regards the content, French manuscripts are homogeneous: The majority of these juridical documents are resolutions issued by various courts concerning inheritance rights, marriage contracts, repayment of debts and land lease. By far the most common manuscript likely to be encountered is the allodial property transfer document. Prior to the 18th century, anyone could seize unoccupied, vacant land and make it theirs provided it was not in use and there was no one to deny permission. Following the French revolution, under Napoleon, the allodial title became the standard in France. It distinguished absolute ownership of land and property from feudal ownership. These documents often have the large title **NAPOLEON** and are always dated. As these fascinating documents, which are hand-written on parchment or paper, are written in old French, they are difficult to read and even more difficult to understand. However, what I like most about them is that each encapsulates a moment in time, an important event for somebody somewhere, even if they are today, little more than decorative objects that can be framed and hung on a wall.

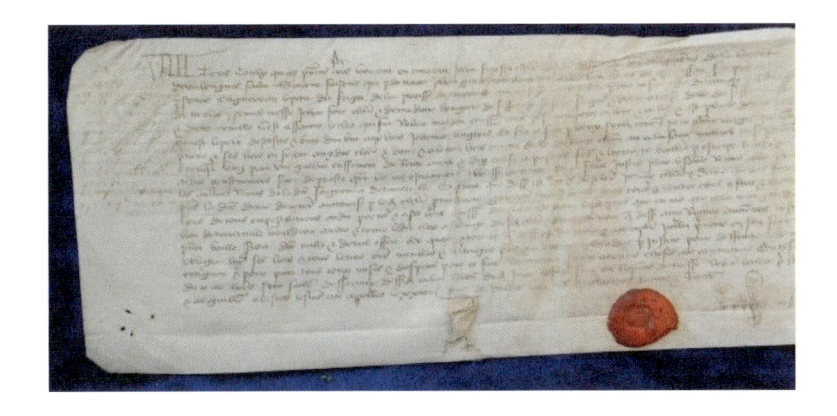

Fig.118. Manuscript on parchment dated 1433

Fig. 119 Fragment of illuminated manuscript

Fig.120. Late period ecclesiastical illuminated manuscript

The principal period for French illuminated manuscripts is from the latter part of the 14th century. Paris at this time was the artistic centre of Europe and influenced illumination for more than a hundred years.

When in the 15th century the French court relocated south, the city of Tours became the main focus for quality manuscript production. Few of these important artworks will remain outside of museums and major collections, but later odd fragments from the lesser centres like Rouen might be found Figures 119 &120.

A painted icon is a flat wooden panel coated with tempera and painted in oils depicting the sacred images of Christ, Mary and Jesus, the saints and angels. Virtually every aspect of the painting is symbolic, like Halos above Christ and the saints and angels, as messengers, have wings. Faces are always portrayed in profile denying the observer the opportunity to make eye contact. The face will also have consistent facial appearances such as large, wide eyes symbolizing looking beyond the material world and outsized ears to enable the hearing of the words of God. The mouth is often disproportionally small to signify empty or harmful words. The icon in Figure 121 is the earliest one I have found. It had a museum label on the back stating it was 14th century but in reality it was a 17thcentury copy, but all the same has an interesting history.

During the sixteenth and the seventeenth century, the treasury at Decani Monastery in modern day Serbia became richer as many objects of art and books were added. It was at this time that manuscripts and icons were copied.

In the late seventeenth century, the monastery was looted for the second time in its history by the Turks who inflicted great damage to both buildings and artworks. This icon has been deliberately defaced by scoring diagonal cut lines and this is likely to have happened at this time.

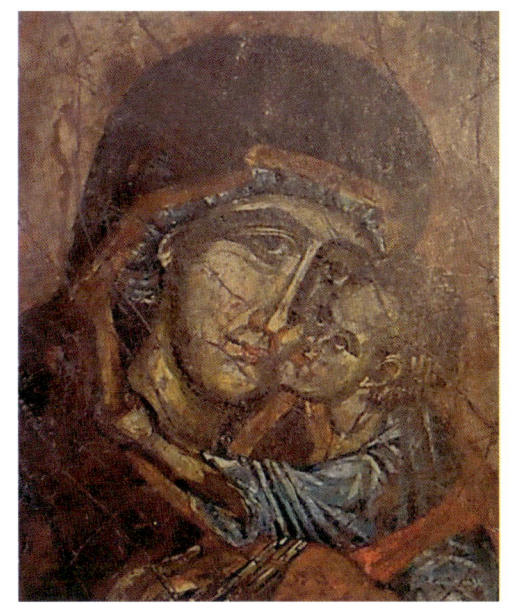

Fig. 121 17th century Serbian icon from the Monastery of Decani.

Fig. 122 18th century Italian. oil painting in ornate frame.

Fig 124 Unknown lady circa 1900

Fig. 123 17th century oil on canvas in the manner of Rembrandt.

Fig.125 Boy and lamb by Gert Hutjens around 1877

Fig. 126 Oil by French artist Claudius Jacquand

Painting has been known since the dawn of history, in fact, for the past 40,000 years. France has rarely been far away from the development of painted art. Perhaps the most famous early images are those from the cave paintings in Languedoc which were daubed on the walls and roof around 16,000 BC. It was not until the latter half of the 15th century following the invasion of Italy that Italian Renaissance art began to make an impression in France. Three hundred years later, the French Revolution and Napoleonic wars brought about the most dramatic changes. Now we see ancient Egyptian influence following Napoleon's campaigns. The idealized wild landscape emerges and reflections of the Middle Ages bring Romanticism to the fore.

In 1874 a collective known as the Anonymous Society of Painters introduced a movement which they called Impressionism and this took Parisian society by surprise. Paris immediately became the hub for the Bohemian artist who uniquely painted life in the city, capturing ordinary people going about their ordinary business. The turn of the century was dominated by the experimentation of colour and now Paris was firmly the world centre for the arts. Whilst the odd 18th or 19th century painting can be found as well as the work of living artists, most of what will be seen at fairs will be country art and of very little value.

Top Tip

Painting or print ? Telling the difference between a print and a painting can be challenging, sometimes even for the experienced if it is under glass. Firstly, it is a good idea to remove the glass, if this is at all possible and look carefully for regular blocks of dots (figure 129). These will confirm the picture is a print. If the painted surface does not have obvious brush marks, it might be a water colour. Look carefully for textured areas, especially variations in roughness. If it has brush marks which logically follow the design, then it is probably an oil painting, (figure 128) but if the brush strokes do not follow the image, then it could well be what is known as an oleograph. These reproductions were printed with faux brush marks and then over-printed with the picture. This is a very simplistic guide as there are also pencil drawings, chalks and acrylics. There are also many different types of prints including woodcuts, engravings, etchings, aquatints, drypoint and lithographs, (figure130) which can sometimes be hand –coloured. (figure 131)

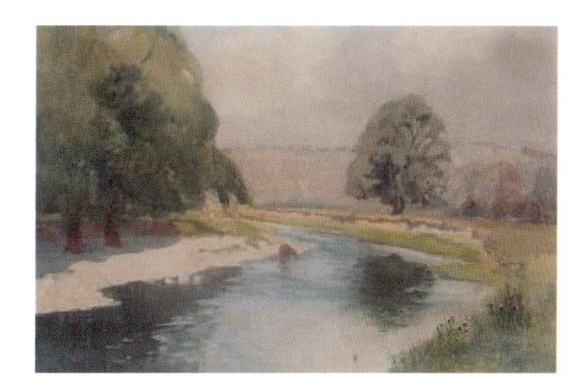

Fig. 127 Four pictures. An oil, a water colour, hand-coloured lithograph and a print.

Fig. 128 Distinctive brush work on an oil.

Fig. 129 Fine dot stippling on print.

Fig. 131 Hand-coloured lithograph.

Fig. 130 Lithograph, signed and numbered.

70

CHAPTER 10

Furniture in the French tradition

Fig.132 French coffer of circa 1660 purchased for 200 euros!.

The earliest form of domestic household furniture was probably the chest. In its simplest humble form it consists of five boards forming the sides and base and a sixth providing the lid. This multi-function container served as storage for clothes, a table and seat. The example above, Fig 132 with its arcading is typical of the mid sixteen hundreds. Another form of furniture in its earliest constituent is that used to contain foodstuffs. Usually of crude construction they are upright cupboard-like pieces known as armoires. Of characteristically squat or rectangular form, they have one or two doors with pierced decoration for the purpose of ventilation. These early 15th 16th century types are unlikely to crop up these days but the example in figure 133 which is 16th century in date was bought at a flea market.

The next most important piece of furniture is the table. Starting life in the medieval period as a simple trestle board, it has evolved very little over the centuries. In France today, the dining table is the most important item of furniture. It is not merely a place to sit and eat, but a place to talk, discuss everyday issues and provide relaxation in lieu of a more comfortable settee. Chairs and benches followed, the latter being most common in rural households.

Fig. 134 18th century corner cupboard

Fig.133 French dairy cupboard with linenfold oak panels. Circa 1550.

Detail of cock's head hinges

Fig. 135 18th century cradle with carved lunette detail.

Fig 136 Breton spindle chair 1900

Fig. 137 Normandy armoire

Fig. 138 Elm bench circa 1800. Below detail of arm

Fig. 139 French country table. Solid oak construction with no hint of any form of embellishment. A base for eating and social interaction. Mid 1800s.

Fig.140 Empire screen

The origins of the armoire for clothes, dates back somewhere before the 16th century. The word *armoire* is a French term that loosely describes any type of wooden cupboard with shelves and surprisingly comes from the Latin 'arma' which translated means tools or perhaps arms. There is a rich and long history of the artistic development of armoires. They rarely bear the signature of the cabinet maker as such, but in fact his signature is in the carving which identifies personal artistic workmanship and the region in which it was made. In their earliest development that is to say from the 16th -18th century, armoires could only be afforded by the wealthy, but as the 19th century progressed, the middle classes added the time-honored closet, as it was often called, to accommodate storage space as well as to provide a decorative focal point to the bedroom. The humble cottage would never have had such a grand piece of furniture. Besides, the armoire was far too high for the low-beamed ceilings of the rural abode. In later years, armoires did find their way into rural cottages; I have seen several which have had their decorative pediments cut-off so as to fit a low-ceilinged bedroom!

The typical French armoire, a few years ago, could be picked up for little more than a hundred pounds. Today, they command prices from several hundred to a thousand euros and more!

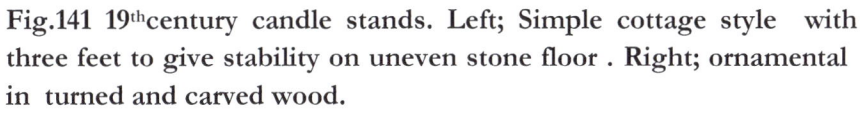

Fig.141 19thcentury candle stands. Left; Simple cottage style with three feet to give stability on uneven stone floor . Right; ornamental in turned and carved wood.

For lighting in domestic homes there were candle stands and these can be frequently found today, and some are surprisingly early. Beds in rural cottages were simple rectangular boxes often with curtains to keep out the draughts; sometimes these were 'trundle beds' designed to be put away into a recess during the day. Grander houses had beds made in exotic woods with carved details of the period and were designed to be seen and admired.

Fig. 142 Girandole wall mirror with two candleholders

Fig.143 Flemish mirror circa 1700

Fig.144 Ormolu cushion mirror 19th. century

Mirrors are another testament to changing fashions. However, in the early days of the mirror, they were not only designed for vanity and decoration, but crucially to reflect the dim glow of night-time candles. To this effect, girandoles were invented as mirrors with candle sconces on each side, but not all are ancient, as the girandole remained popular as a decoration, particularly in ormolu bronze, throughout the 19th and well into the 20th century Figure 142. Some of the earliest examples I have seen have been gilded wood and plaster, but these tend to command high prices.

The ornate carved and gilded mirror in Figure 143 is late 17th century and probably Flemish. A particular style of mirror during the 19th century was the six piece cushion form with ormolu decoration, often in a loose rococo style. (Figure 144.)

Other, more easily affordable types are the crested mirrors with highly carved central ornamentation, the rectangular mirror with decorative borders and D-shaped over mantel mirrors. These late 19th early 20th century types are very popular with interior decorators today, but as they lack quality and are invariably chipped and have missing gesso, they are often painted and then distressed and as a result can look very acceptable in modern surroundings.

Top Tip

Antique or reproduction?

Firstly consider the type of wood used for the item in question as wood types were often standard for classes of furniture. Early furniture prior to the 17th century was mostly oak, but in parts of France, and Normandy in particular, elm was widely used for tables, benches and stools. By the early 1700s, fruitwood and walnut often replaced oak for country furniture. By the middle of the century, mahogany made its appearance but on account of its high price, was only used for quality pieces. By the 19th century rosewood, satin wood and exotic species like tulip and Kingwood were used for marquetry and inlay on pieces of the finest quality. Pine was the reserve for country furniture and widely used throughout the 19th and 20th centuries.

The finish on a piece of furniture can help date it, but beware, many a fine item has been stripped and re-polished at a later date. But in essence, early examples will have little more than wax and a great patina. From the 18th century shellac was widely used until it was joined by varnish in the mid-1800s.

Finally, it is important to remember machine-made joinery post-dates 1860 and so it is necessary to closely examine components such as dovetail joints in drawers, spindles and turned parts. Machine-made furniture will always be precise whereas an early antique will not be perfect; it will rarely be symmetrical or evenly matched. Close scrutiny will reveal these differences which are the result of hand-making

17th centry child's chair   Fruitwood and oak dining room chairs around 1800

Bentwood 1880/1910   Button-back leather 1900   Art Deco club
.   Fig. 145 Some common chair types   20th century

CHAPTER 11

Boxes and chests

A box is a lidded, wooden container distinguished from its larger cousin, the chest, primarily by its smaller size, although there can be an overlap between the two.

Boxes have been made for more than two thousand years; their popularity has never waned as containers for every conceivable object. Some of the more common uses have resulted in various distinguishable types, such as; trinket box, bible box, candle box, money box, writing box, jewelry box, knife box, sewing box, as well as tea caddies, snuff and patch boxes and an enormous range of product boxes in tin and cardboard. Many of these are self-explanatory and readily recognizable, such as the sloping-lid construction of the writing box, but when it comes to the bible box, while many will have been used to house the family bible, the term now applies to a flat boarded box commonly carved with simple arcading, lunettes, and other geometric patterns like the item in Figure 156 which dates to circa 1680.

Boxes have been made in a vast variety of materials from gold and silver to pewter and brass or in wood from oak to exotic hardwoods, papier-mâché, tortoiseshell and lacquer to porcelain & pottery.

Although wooden boxes are often referred to as one of the more primitive forms of furniture, they can be seen as representative of the entire history of cabinet making, exemplifying changing styles, construction methods, and materials. Examples include relatively crude nailed boxes from the Age of Oak to copiously carved 18th century masterpieces, constructed with dovetails or frame-and-panel joinery; boxes with applied moldings and turnings; later boxes from the 17th and 18th centuries, made of walnut and other woods, often inlaid with coloured veneers. In the 19th century veneering techniques led to the very popular Tunbridge type wares, a generic term for the inlaying of exotic woods.

Fig. 146 Empire box with ormolu fittings 1860

Fig.147 Folk art box dated 1775

Fig 148 Inlaid satinwood tea caddy

Fig. 149 casket with Paris scene.

Fig. 150 exotic wood inlay

Fig.151 Early 19th century candle box

152 Casket with high relief mythological.　Fig. 153 novelty casket around 1900

Other materials such as ivory, mother-of-pearl, shagreen and curled paper were popular mediums for decorative boxes, particularly tea caddies. There are also a great variety of more contemporary boxes made for entirely modern objects such as military, scientific or medical instruments.

France has long enjoyed a particular relationship with the box, particularly the tourist- based product. Boxes made for special events go right back to the early 18th century when pilgrims visiting the holy shrines at Lourdes, Paris, Lisieux, Nevers, Paray le Monial, Lyon, La Salette, Avignon, Carcassonne etc. brought about a demand for something to take home. Artists made objects that allowed pilgrims to commemorate their visit. The earliest containers were boxes in ivory, ormolu or even precious metals made as reliquary containers to hold tiny fragments of bone from venerated saints. Later boxes were printed with scenes of Cathedrals, Basilicas and other sacred sites. By the 19th century tourists were flocking to France and in particular Paris and this gave rise to the small glass-sided ormolu jewellery box with the local landmark printed in colour on the lid, the most popular was of course the Eiffel tower. (Figure 149) But most major towns had their own particular tourist attraction printed on souvenir boxes and these were sold in vast numbers and are still plentiful today.

Fig.154 Ormolu box with pastoral detail. Paris 1865

Fig. 155 Cloisonné box 1900

Fig.156 Carved bible box circa 1680

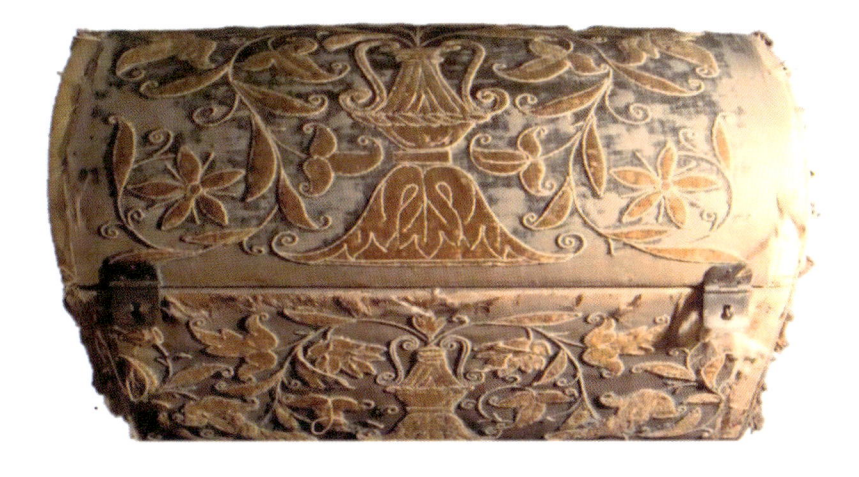

Fig.157 Embroidered casket circa 1680/1700

Fig. 158 Brass-studded leather on wood trunk circa 1800

Fig. 159 Pine mule chest circa 1860-80

CHAPTER 12

Clocks

When the spring-powered clock was invented somewhere around 1510 in Germany, it gave rise to an acceleration of clock-making. Having said this, few examples from this time exist outside of museums. Generally the earliest French clocks that might be found date from the early 18th century and even these will normally command high prices. Early longcase clocks are not often encountered at flea markets, although brass faces can occasionally be found. In their day they were reserved only for the wealthy, being expensive at that time; bracket clocks of this period are even scarcer. The most prolific period of clock-making was from the mid-18th century when clocks began to have a glass front door and ornate ormolu decoration on top, often depicting classical figures.

The beginning of the 19th century saw the Gothic style emerge and now we find time pieces taking the form of cathedrals, basilicas and often with the working mechanism exposed. The latter are known as skeleton clocks.

Clock design has always followed fashion and never more so than during the Art Nouveau and Art Deco periods. During this time we see the use of heavy marble and onyx and accompanying garnitures.

The quintessential French time-piece is the carriage clock which was first made in France by Abraham Louis Breguet for military use during the Napoleonic wars and, shortly after, produced in large numbers by every respectable clockmaker. By 1830 French carriage clocks were being exported to England in large quantities.

These were spring-driven rather than pendulum, with a platform escapement visible through the glass top. They were designed specifically for travelling and usually have a carrying handle.

By far the most common clock during the 19th century was the longcase Comptoise clock. Thought to have originated in Morbier, in the French region of Comté, they were soon being made in virtually every town in France and identifiable by the town name on the dial. These clocks had inverted verge escapements in iron or wood frames and large stone or iron weights and large brass pendulums which swung between the movement and dial. They are generally housed in a gently tapering wooden case, sometimes grained to imitate fine woods and quite often brightly painted as in our Figure 167. Brass pediments had details which included baskets of flowers, praying angels and classical anthemion, a flower-like design.

Fig. 160 Brass sun dial dated 1706.

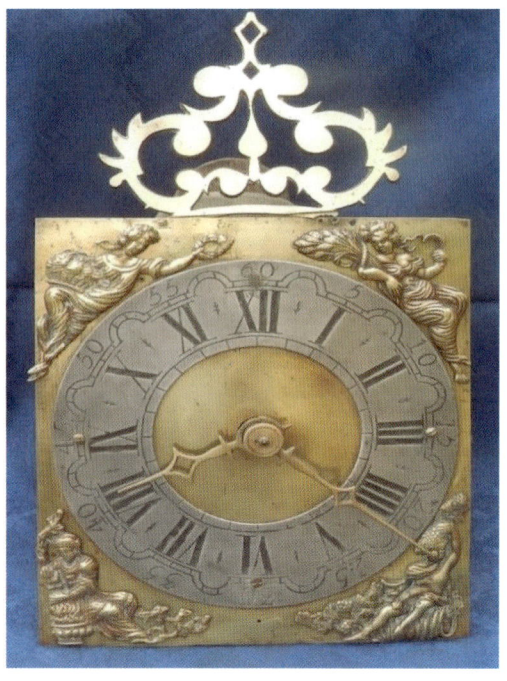

Fig. 161 Longcase clock with ormolu. spandrels around 1800.

Fig.162 Black Forest hand-painted on wood, around 1840.

Fig.163 Toleware painted kitchen clock.

Fig.164 Various good quality ormolu -cased clocks

Clocks from Germany were imported during the 18th century, the most popular being the Black Forest, painted dial, 30- hour wall clock. These basically simple time-pieces, in their earliest form, had wooden cases and dial and were always very brightly painted as in Figure 162. They can be frequently picked up at markets, and for a modest sum.

Fig. 165 Ormolu mantel clock Paris 1900

Fig166 Age of Jazz Art Deco clock.

Fig.167 Normandy Comptoise longcase clock mid-1800s.

88

Fig.168 French Napoleon 111 mantel clock. Ormolu and marble around 1900

Fig. 169 20th century yellow marble by good Paris retailer

CHAPTER 13

From the Orient: Chinese and Asian art.

France, like most of Europe, has enjoyed the unique art of China for almost four hundred years. Everyone knows the name Ming, which to many is considered synonymous with great value. However, the only really valuable pieces are Imperial wares made for the Emperor. Such pieces were exquisitely decorated and signed with the reign mark of the emperor and made specifically for use at court and are rarely found in the west. There are, however, good opportunities for finding decent examples of Ming period export ware. Because there are so many copies and reproductions around, it is necessary to be familiar with the genuine, but unfortunately the only way to familiarise oneself is by visiting museums, and if at all possible, handling specimens. In this small book I can only illustrate a few examples and narrate a short history of this extensive and exciting field of antiques.

In China an Imperial porcelain factory was established at Jingdezhen at the very beginning of the Ming Dynasty (1369-1644) These early examples closely follow archaic traits, but the quality now became less bold, if more refined.

A century later, during the reign of the Emperor Wanli, porcelain production had become large-scale and was now being exported to practically every corner of the World. Like most parts of Europe, in France, decorative Chinese wares were imported in large quantities. The new taste for what was to become known in the west as Chinoiserie was to have an immense impact on architectural design and soon led to the emergence of the rococo style.

Fig.170 Group of Chinese Ming and Kangxi porcelain 16th-18th century.

Fig. 171 17th/18th century blue and white Chinese porcelain.

Fig.172 Inspiration for the English willow pattern. 19th century.

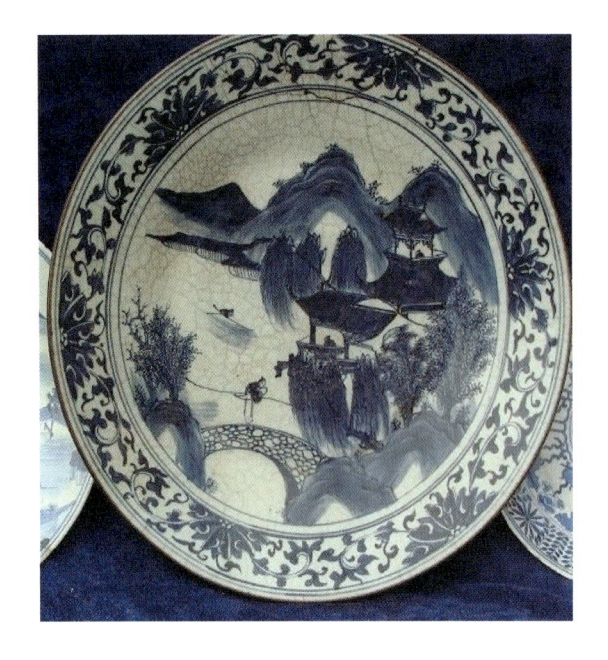

Fig.173 1800s crackle glaze charger.   Fig. 174 ginger jar 1800

There was no break in the ceramic tradition when the Ming were overthrown by the Manchus in 1644 in what became the Ch'ing dynasty.

By the early 1800's, China remained isolated from trade with the outside world. The Chinese port of Canton was the sole vehicle for export with the West, and although porcelains and silks were filtering into Europe in large quantities, the principal export was now tea.

Fig. 176 Imperial yellow bowl with anhua engraving.

Fig.175 Crackle glaze monochrome

Fig.177 Massive Japanese Imari jardinière

Up until the 1900s, virtually all Chinese art was specifically made for export. Following the Opium wars and the Boxer rebellion, the occupation of Peking by the allied army became the scene of plunder and destruction on a large scale. One correspondent, the French commander, General de Compte d'Herisson witnessed his own troops looting the Summer Palace, temples, and elegant shops of Peking and noted how they were loading wagons with porcelains, ivories, silver and gold, jewels, furs, silk, and paintings. Another observer described the event as the biggest looting excursion since the days of Pizarro'. Large quantities of Imperial porcelain and other art very quickly came on the market and by 1912 following the founding of the Chinese Republic, the collecting of Chinese art became fashionable and several important collections started to take shape. Oriental pottery and porcelain often has reign marks on the bases and when it comes to Japanese pieces, reign marks and regional place of manufacture marks can virtually always be accepted as of the period. However, when it comes to Chinese pottery and porcelain these are to be viewed with great caution. It was during the early fifteenth century Yongle period when the addition of painting reign marks on ceramics was first practiced, the mark usually consisted of the reign title of the emperor and the name of the dynasty. Unfortunately marks of earlier periods have been widely used over the centuries, mostly apocryphal but sometimes to honour a certain ware and likely often to deceive. Determining a genuine piece which is mark and period, involves not just the calligraphy, but knowledge of both the shape and form of the vessel and vibrancy and quality of painting.

The end of the 19th century saw China and Japan open to the west and following the London, Vienna and finally in 1878, the Paris exhibitions, the taste for Chinoiserie and the new Japanese saw a flood of Oriental art being exported to the west and other parts of the World. I have mainly focused on pottery and porcelain but in much smaller numbers, wood carvings, silks and bronzes have come out of China for hundreds of years and from Japan, fine ivories and stunning 19th century bronzes. Few of these categories of Oriental art will be discovered in flea markets today, but there are still a few sleeping treasures to be found as can be seen from my examples in this chapter.

Fig.179 Chinese 6-charter mark of Cheng Hua

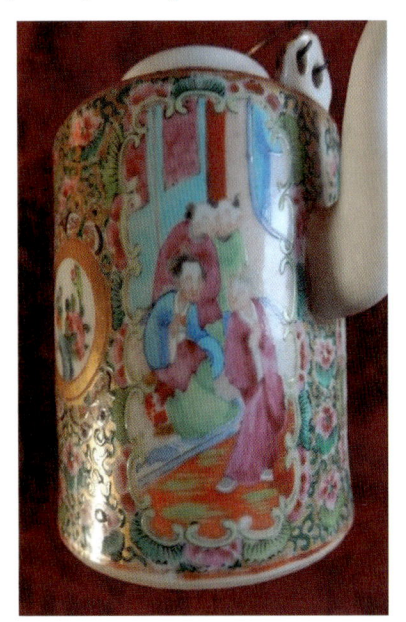

Fig. 178 Chinese Canton ware 19th century.

Fig. 180 Front and back of a 19th century Japanese Kutani dish with seal mark on base.

Fig. 181 Bronze figure 17th century with traces of gilding.

Fig. 182 Tibetan bronze with concealed scroll inside.

Fig. 183 Japanese solid bronze of Hotei, signed by Tokyo School artist. Around 1900

Fig. 184 Japanese lacquer cabinet 1900

Fig.185 Chinese Ruyi sceptre.

Fig 186 Chinese jade snuff bottle

Fig. 187 Canton enamel 1880s

Fig.188 Japanese inlaid frame 1900

Top Tip

Chinese or Japanese. People often ask 'How do you know if a bronze is Chinese or Japanese as the two often look so very similar? ' I tend to reply 'I just know the difference when I see it', but in order to build that instinctive knowledge it is necessary to see as many examples as possible. In the meantime, a reasonable assessment can be made by going through a check list.

When it comes to the metallic nature and surface patination, they will invariably be very similar, but the first clue regarding our examples is that the left-hand vase has a gold-splashed surface which is characteristic of Chinese work. Both vessels have decoration, but the production techniques differ. The Chinese vase has design elements cut in to the body of the work, whereas the Japanese example has bold raised ornament. The handles and feet on the latter are very decorative figural embellishments, but the Chinese vase has simple archaic representations of handles.

Fig.189 Chinese bronze vessel 18th century.
.

Fig 190 Japanese bronze vessel 19th century

Both have strong Buddhist symbolism, however, such motifs like dogs of foe, dragons and tigers were popular in both Japan and China, so do not generally help distinguish between the two cultures.

Generally speaking, Chinese art tends to look back in awe at its ancestors, copying artistic and symbolic ornament in reverence rather than replication or imitation. The emphasis will be very much on symbolic representation, with little or no inventive elements. Japanese art on the other hand is far more playful, inventive, depicting aspects of everyday life, in particular, natural elements such as trees, flowers and the animal World. There will still often be aspects of archaism, but far less formal.

When it comes to makers signatures and marks of reverence, Chinese examples will almost always have apocryphal marks, not necessarily to deceive but of little help in dating. Japanese bronzes on the other hand, if marked, will mostly be genuine and will invariably be the artists name or place of manufacture.

Like most classes of Oriental art, there are forgeries and one area which has been prolific in recent years, are copies of Tokyo School bronzes which are usually signed and very difficult to distinguish from the early twentieth century originals.

Fig 191 Japanese mark on bronze figure around 1900

CHAPTER 14

Antiquities and tribal art

Fig. 192 Roman drinking cups, Etruscan carving and Roman coins

Before the 16th century there is little evidence for the collecting of antiquities, although we know some Romans two thousand years ago had collections of bygone artifacts. When it came to collecting antiquities in more recent years, France was, from the very beginning, ahead of the game. In the early 16th century, French ambassadors working in Rome sent back antiquities to collectors at court and in particular, to the Kings collection at Fontainebleau. Eminent politicians like Jean Du Bellay, who was obsessed with the desire to transfer cultural and architectural objects and ideology from ancient Rome back to France, shipped back quantities of artifacts and even commissioned excavations in order to locate more treasures buried in the ground.

The European attraction to classical antiquities didn't really take off until the 18th century and at that time was reserved entirely for the upper classes. It was a by-product of a classical education which included Greek and Roman architecture, mythology and Latin. This introduction to antiquities was often supplemented by 'The Grand Tour' visiting the ancient ruins of Pompeii and Herculaneum, Rome, Athens and the great pyramids of Egypt. Visibility of artifacts played an important role in stirring a need to collect. Museums, excavations and early collectors were willing to show off their new-found knowledge, backed up by artifactual evidence. The upper classes also had libraries which contained antiquarian books by the likes of William Hamilton who published a catalogue of his extensive collection in 1766. These new antiquarians had access to the 'Augustan Age of English literature' which explored Rome and its writers, and for their houses, they were quick to commission classical-inspired architecture and in particular, Wedgewood interpretation for their interiors.

Fig.193 Bronze age flint arrow head around 1000BC

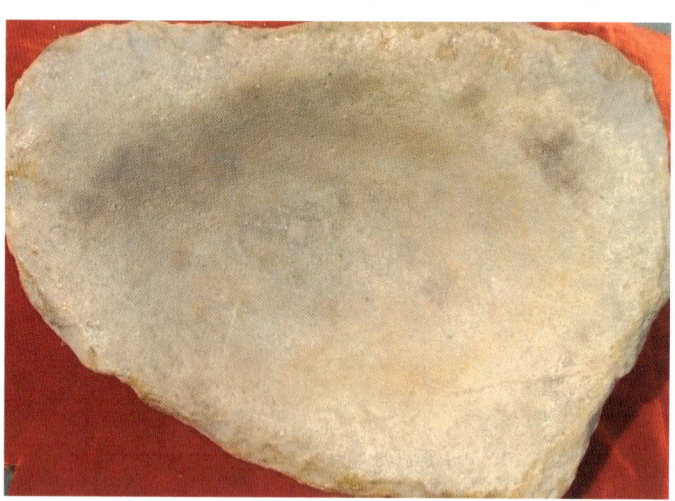

Fig. 194 Neolithic saddle quern around 4000 BC

Fig. 196 Front and back of Egyptian scarab incised with hieroglyphs.

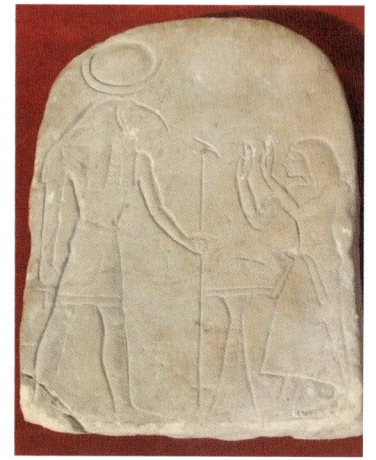

Fig. 195 Egyptian funerary stele

Fig. 199 Roman Ointment
Fig 198 Roman pot. 2nd century.   flask. 3rd century AD

Fig.197 Greek terracotta figure 2nd century BC.

As a retired archaeologist, I have an obvious advantage when it comes to spotting genuine antiquities for there are so many copies and reproductions, particularly when it comes to Egyptian artifacts. For the past two hundred years tourists have been visiting historical sites around the world, and naturally keen to bring back a souvenir or two. Demand soon outstripped the quantity of antiquities available for sale and so the fakers were quick to fill the gap. People are usually surprised to learn that a genuine Roman pottery vessel, sixteen hundred years old can be worth little more than a hundred pounds, and a flint arrow head which might be 4000 years old can be bought for as little as 10 euros. I think this all illustrates that the majority of antiquities available in French flea markets will have little monetary value, but they are fascinating items to collect. Also it is important to remember that antiquities are not just artifacts but cultural and social evidence of people from the past and their real value is what they can tell us when found in situ in the ground. Just imagine holding a 2,000 year old pot, your hands are making direct contact with the ancient past, the person who originally owned it, their life was so very different to ours of today. But the other thing which puzzles me is where such items have been during the past two millennia. I think in almost all cases they have been discovered in the ground by someone, somewhere and filtered through the market place, sometimes across continents to end up in a French flea market in the twenty first century.

Fig. 200 Greek or Etruscan bronze dagger. 1st century BC

Tribal art is a direct continuation of the antiquity of artifacts. Whilst we are not talking about objects thousands of years old, they are part of the material culture of indigenous peoples whether from the African Continent, Australasia or Oceanic Islands. The 19th century was the key period when, European collector explorers returned with artifacts which shed new light on how indigenous people lived, their cultural practices, religion and iconography. Many are now where they should be, in museums, but there are plenty to be found at the flea market today, albeit, mostly comparatively modern and made as tourist souvenirs.

Fig.201 Chancay pottery Figure

Fig. 202 Teotihuacan Inca temple tile.

Fig. 203 African pottery Mangbetu cup.

Top Tip

Before buying it is essential to train one's eye and look at every facet of an artifact. I will always ask questions of an antiquity: is it really old and does it have a patina, that is to say the alteration of a surface through prolonged use or oxidation, especially if it is likely to have spent time in the ground; was this created to serve a use or purpose and does it function correctly for that purpose or, on closer inspection, is it actually unsuitable for the purpose and no more than an attractive ornament? If it is the latter then be cautious as it might well have been made for the tourist market. Finally, provenance is vital when it comes to antiquities and items which are not self-explanatory. Ask questions of the seller, he or she may not be willing to discuss where or how they came across the item, but I often find a vender is proud of the piece and wants to tell you all they know about it, even if their beliefs are not credible or strictly accurate. Any information adds so much to the historical value.

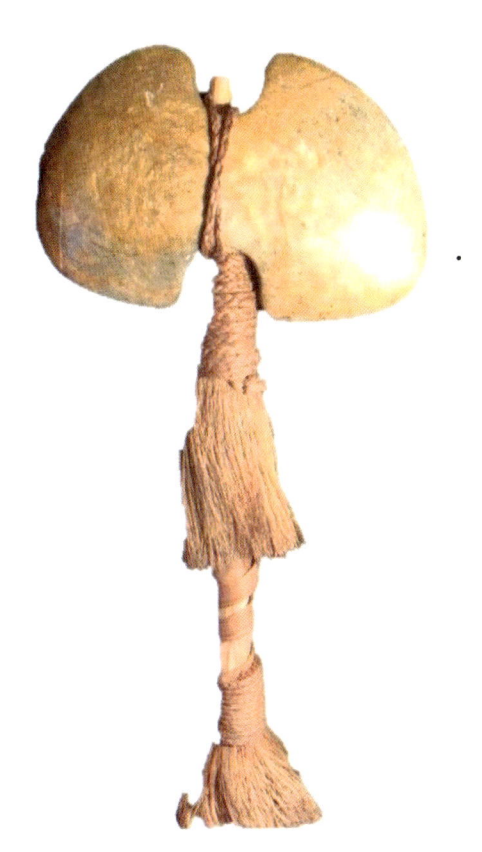

Fig.204 Oceanic ceremonial axe.

Fig. 205 Rare jade mace New Caledonia

Fig.206 African wood head rest 20th century

Fig.207 Solomon Islands bird-head bowl.

CHAPTER 15

Samplers and beadwork

Fig. 208 French beadwork dated 1840

From the late 18th century, girls from as young as seven, learned needle craft from their mothers and grandmothers and probably from each other. It was an essential part of female education that would demonstrate her sewing skills and attract a husband. The well-to-do household would provide silk, wool and beads which were very expensive compared to threads. The less affluent home would possess only threads of wool. As well as creating colourful pictures of houses, churches and countryside, the girls learnt numbers and the alphabet which they set out with immaculate skill within floral or geometric borders. If the work was good, it showed off the young girls sewing skills and her level of education when seen by a suitable bachelor on the principal room walls.

Samplers were generally rectangular, cross stitch or needlepoint done directly on fabric, frequently fairly course linen or cotton. Later examples were often stitched onto punched paper templates.

Modern day tambour work is still used for creating decorative beadwork and embroidery, the very best work is produced in France for the fashion industry and is still taught at the Ecole Lesage in Paris.

Top Tip

Generally the value of any sampler will depend on two factors; the quality of the silks or beads and the imagery. Early examples often have a religious theme and may be worth less than a 19th century example with a map, house or church. The most collectable samplers are those with amusing subjects, perhaps a wild animal with unrealistic features. The name and age of the girl is also desirable and more so if she has an amusing name like Fanny Joynt as on the Figure 209 below. The topping on the cake will be a date; the earlier the better.

Fig.209 Sampler around 1800   Fig.210 French sampler around 1900

Fig.211 Colourful French sampler dated 1910

Fig. 212 Machine loomed design after William Morris.

CHAPTER 16

Textiles, Lace, Costume and Fashion

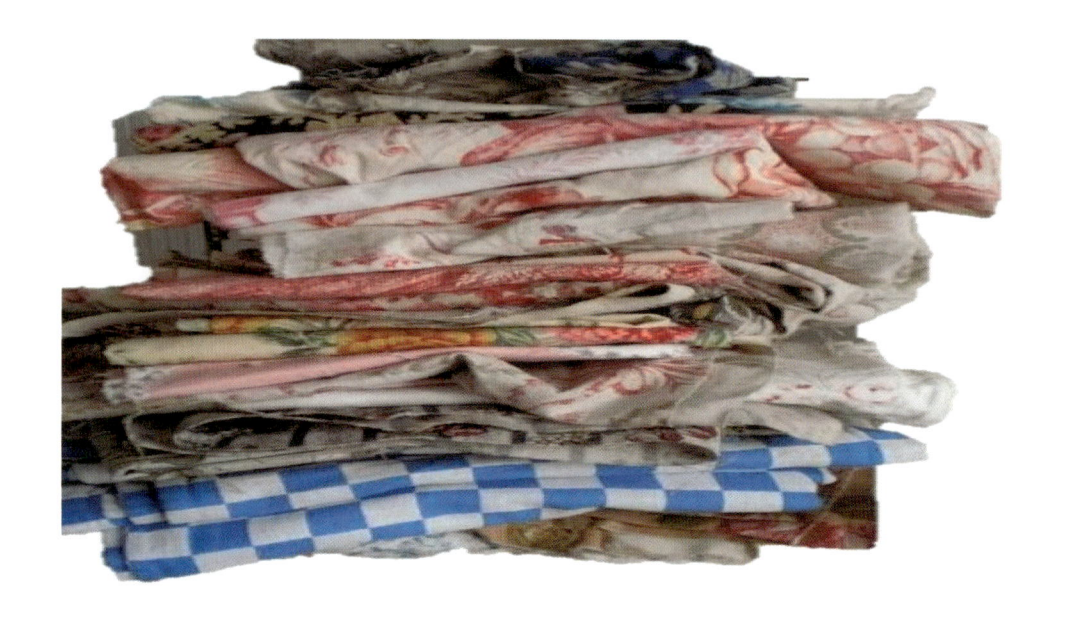

The need or choice to wear clothing is solely a hominoid characteristic of human society. Originating in the use of animal skins to protect against inclement weather conditions; its roots are believed to be the result of migration of peoples to colder climates. Several centuries before the Industrial Revolution, the wealthy elements of society were the singular reason for new textile invention and production. By the late 16th century patterned silk, damasks, velvets and brocades, often embellished with precious gold or silver threads heralded a new wave of textile manufacture in France. However, this momentous development now required skilled weavers and a considerable investment in equipment and raw materials. These early textiles are rarely found today except in 'high end' specialist shops. However, the 17th century altar cushion illustrated on Figure 213 was one of two which I found at a flea market and purchased for a few euros!

Fig. 213 Altar cushion around 1660

By the 17th century, brightly patterned cotton fabric from India was becoming popular in France. So prevalent was this new colourful textile, that France temporarily banned its importation. By 1760 the embargo had been lifted and the colourful textiles were being produced by the firm of **Royale de Jouy**, near Paris and a new chapter in French textile design began.

Toile de Jouy or more commonly referred to as simply toile, is an off-white textile background on which a repeated pattern depicting allegorical and pastoral scenes were printed in reds, blues, greens, browns and black.(Figures 214 &215.) Toile textiles were in the main, produced as curtains and bed hangings and general upholstery and by the 19th century the industrial output was massive. With over 30,000 designs, Toile de Jouy continues to be popular today. The Industrial Revolution played a major role in transforming the production and consumption of textiles from the early 1800s. The production of new textiles did more to forward the factory system in Europe than any other industry. It was the necessity to speed up production for the textile industry, that the steam engine perfected by James Watt, was applied to the power loom. Now, more plain and patterned material could be mass produced, cheaply and available to a greater proportion of society. France continued to be

Fig. 214 18th century toile printed in madder red.

Fig. 215 19th/20thcentury toile.

the leading source for luxury dress and furnishing silks during the nineteenth century, and even today, it is a forerunner in Europe.

During the early 1500s, a form of openwork fabric was made for enhancing collars, cuffs and catholic vestments. It wasn't until the closing years of the 16th century that there was a sudden and rapid development in the field of lace making. At this time it was no more than a cottage industry producing doilies, tablecloths and clothing.

Much like textiles, it was the Industrial revolution which changed the nature of lace making. Now, there was a great demand which could not be met by the cottage industry and from the 1760s the bobbin net machine made possible, complex lace designs in large quantities, and making it accessible to all elements of society. Handmade lace never died out completely, and even today is widely made by hobbyists. Values of fine hand-made lace can be very high, whereas machine-made items can be bought quite cheaply.

216-218 Examples of antique lace.

Fig. 219 Dowry bed sheet monograms

Monograms were embroidered initials, sometimes embellished with flowers, which were sewn on French bed linen in the 19th and early 20th centuries. Well-to-do households had pure linen sheets whereas the poorer elements of society had coarser hemp sheets or a mixture of the two. Despite the differences in quality of the bed linen, the incredibly high standard of monogram sewing remained the same. From a young age a girl would, invariably with the help of her mother, create her trousseau, the package of linens which consisted of up to twelve sheets, hand and dish towels, napkins, tablecloths and lace. Before she reached her teens, she would have meticulously embroidered all her dowry ready for marriage. Of course, at this stage she had no idea who she might marry so only embroidered her own initial, her intended husbands initial would be entwined with hers during the customary courtship period. The dowry custom was in essence, a material way of making a statement of marital commitment and creating protection for a long life together. The complete dowry, finished before the wedding, went with her to her new home. A sheet or other fabric with only one initial sadly suggests a girl never did find her perfect husband.

Few early costumes survive outside of museums and those that do, are generally pieces kept for sentimental reasons such as wedding veils, accessories and baby christening gowns. Fashion trends in the first half of the 20th century were dominated by the Paris fashion houses such as Paquin, Jacques Doucet and Paul Poiret. From the 1920s Gabrielle Chanel took centre stage and by the late 1940s Christian Dior began to steal the limelight. Any of these labels on a piece of Haute Couture costume will demand a very high price, but even so, we have heard of such pieces occasionally turning up at French flea markets. Styles have always kept up with fashion. The boyish drop wasted dresses of the 1920s deliberately sought to hide the female form whereas by the 1930s, the bias-cut gowns with their emphasis on cling to curves abruptly reinvented femininity. In the postwar years, there was a vogue for loose-fitting garments which were now made in large numbers as off- the-peg couture. Ready-to-wear clothes will always be much more affordable and can still be discovered in all sorts of places including flea markets, vide greniers and vintage clothing shops.

Fig.220 Cotton dress around 1920

Fig. 221 Around 1900 satin and needlework

Fig. 222 1950s off- the- peg couture.

Fig. 223 Art Deco jacket with stylish pockets. 1930s

There has been much speculation as to when humans first covered their heads; the tradition certainly goes back several thousand years. Early head wear was undoubtedly more a necessity in order to protect from injury rather than a mere accessory, although in early Dynastic Egypt, this might not have always been the case as head wear was a symbol of status.

The ubiquitous French beret is similar to and possibly has its origins in comparable head-wear worn by Bronze Age man three thousand years ago. By the middle ages, it was a utilitarian protective hat worn by French shepherds and was only adopted by the military in the 1880s. By the 1920s, the soft wool brimless cap was worn by men and women alike to ward off cold, wind and rain, but it was mostly considered working class attire and became synonymous with the French onion seller.

Fig. 224 Summer floral bonnet 1940s

Fig. 225 Vintage hats first half of the twentieth century

Today, it is often worn by women as a fashion accessory. Following the strict canon law of the 13th century, the French Catholic Church decreed that women must have their heads covered, and whilst this law no longer applies, many French women still wear silk bonnets for this occasion. Simple shepherdess hats were soon followed by bonnets. At first in cotton or silk and later in straw and other fabrics, by the 18th century they had become standard wear for all echelons of society.

By the 18th century hats had become the singular accessory to draw attention to the wearers face, their styles now followed and sometimes inspired fashions of the day. By the mid-19th century the bonnet had expanded to vast proportions, now framing the female face but hiding her side profile. Fashion hats as accessories reached their most flamboyant in the closing years of the century.

Fashion plates are interesting documents which provide a unique vision of the dressing habits and tastes of middle class women and the aspirations they had for higher society models. The 18th century fashion plate was usually coloured by hand, but by the second half of the 19th century, coloured lithographs were being produced in periodicals and women's magazines. In France, "La Galerie des Modes" was a leader in fashion plate publication. At that time we also see foreign fashions, dressing accessories and hairstyles showcased in the popular french magazines of the day and distributed right across Europe. These designs charter the ready-to-wear fashion industry throughout the nineteenth and into the early years of the 20th century.

Shortly, photography would herald the end of the fashion plate when magazines would change to the new technology, offering a more realistic portrayal of fashion for mass-media demand.

Figs 226-228 Fashion plates. Left; April 1900. Right; early 20th century

CHAPTER 17

Style and the new order; Art Nouveau

Art Nouveau, along with its continental cousin, Jugendstil is an ornamental style movement applied to the decorative arts across Europe and the United States from 1890-1910. It was a reaction against 19th century imitative historicism which had dominated the decorative arts for decades. Art Nouveau style embraces all forms of applied arts, including metalwork, furniture, household utensils, fabrics, jewellery, graphic art, lighting and architecture. It employs a noticeably organic style using natural forms, mostly flowers, plants and insects linked by long, sinuous, curvilinear ornament.

Clay for potting was the perfect medium for the Art Nouveau aesthetic movement. It has a malleable organic nature which lends itself to the artist potters to shape into sinewy lines. The introduction of new glazing techniques added another new dimension and now pottery was intended to be more than just decorative. The vast numbers of dinner services and tea sets, flower vases and jardinières, whilst of aesthetic beauty, were also utilitarian. France was not slow to adopt the new developing movement. In 1903 Alphonse Cytere set up an art studio in Rambervillers which produced ceramics often designed by prominent artists of the Ecole de Nancy such as Bussiere, Gruber, Jeandelle and Majorelle. These innovators specialized in iridescent glazes on organic forms. Such examples are not likely to be found for modest sums at flea markets but pieces by less important artists are still plentiful and examples from other European countries can also end up on a market stall. There is still enormous opportunity to discover metal-ware at flea markets. The most common of this period will be in the Jugendstil style and whilst there are many French examples, the most numerous and successful pieces are from the German company of WMF (Württembergische Metallwarenfabrik). Founded in 1880, it was the world's largest producer and exporter of household metal ware during the Art Nouveau period. Their output specialised in every day, yet ornamental household items in pewter, silver plate, copper and brass. However, prices fluctuate from time to time and it is true to say their popularity has recently declined.

Fig. 229 Art Nouveau bread dish around 1900   Fig. 230 Typical pin dish in brass.

Fig. 231 Art Nouveau basin and bowl

Fig. 232 Oak chest with Honesty pattern carving

Fig. 233 The famous WMF mark

Fig. 234 Pewter with mistletoe.

Fig. 235 Secessionist pottery vase

CHAPTER 18

Sculpture and the Belle Époque

The *Belle Époque* (Beautiful Era) was a period in French and Belgian history that is conventionally dated as starting after the Franco-Prussian War in the late 1800s and ending at the beginning of World War I in 1914. It was a period characterized by a sudden optimism and in some quarters, prosperity. It marks the foundation of a new appreciation of Impressionist art. It is a cultural and technological high point which led to an affluence which created an environment ripe for invention and experimentation. In Paris this is seen not only in its architecture but also the city encouraged the visual arts, music, theatre and literature to flourish. The likes of the Moulin Rouge fed the hunger for the *risqué* and a new Bohemian lifestyle, when the "Chat Noir" opened in 1881. The iconic Eiffel Tower, built as the grand entrance to the 1889 World's Fair, became, and is still to this day, the symbol of the city.

The Belle Époque is notable for its great diversity of decorative elements: the architectural friezes and stucco work, faux stone effects, moulded busts and grotesques, and decorative ironwork. For the home, sculptors were producing exquisite busts in bronze, spelter, terracotta and plaster. Furniture and ceramics and, in Nancy, Emile Gallé was making glass. The likes of Carlier, Carrier, Thomas Cartier, Daum, Emile Galle, Larche, Louis Majorelle, Moreau and Villeneuve to mention but a few, worked in Paris and Nancy during these early years.

Fig. 236 Busts in plaster left, Spelter right.

Fig.237 Spelter figurine - music.

Fig. 238 Children in playful poses were popular.   Fig. 239 Iron door knocker.

Synonymous with the Beaux Art movement are the wonderful busts. The very best were modelled and then cast in bronze. Those of lesser quality were made in spelter and those for the masses were fashioned in terra cotta or plaster. I personally feel that the humble plaster versions from the turn of the century, by the very nature of their fabric and colouring, merge the best of the Beaux Arts and Art Nouveau styles. (Figure 236 &237)

Subjects mainly reflect the sensuous energy of youth and are often, especially in the case of female busts, more about personality than beauty. They exemplify a romantic hunger for purity mixed with the Gallic desire for plenty. The time was also a frivolous and playful period as can be seen by the accompanying illustrations (Figure 238).

Fig. 241 Brass ornament with caduceus- 'horn of plenty'.

Fig.240 Glazed terracotta pottery wall cherub.

Fig 242 Belle Époque candelabra

Fig. 243 Bronze Jeanne d'Arc plaque

Top Tip

The reproduction of glass from this period began in the second quarter of the 20th century and due to the demand for genuine pieces, peaked in the 1980s. Pieces by Emile Galle are the most copied, but there are several clues to help distinguish genuine pieces from the fake. Often, the overall decoration is just wrong; it might be spread unevenly over the entire vessel, or it might be too dark or just lacking lustre. The neck on a reproduction is often entirely covered in overlay creating an imbalance of design. The signature would normally be on the neck, although this is not always the case, and fakes often have signatures which are too large. Another trick of the fakers is to make a respectable reproduction of the type which is marked Tip Galle look genuine by removing the word 'Tip'.

Fig. 244 Large ormolu jardinière or table centerpiece with playful cherubs.

CHAPTER 19

Art Deco

Art Deco was an international style that dominated architecture and the decorative arts from the mid-1920s until the start of the Second World War in 1939, although elements of the style continued into the 1950s.

Art deco style is an amalgam of many different decorative influences including Art Nouveau, Cubism and neo-classical elements. It sought to introduce a modern vision that embraced technological advances, yet looked back to ancient cultures. The movement employed geometric shapes and devices like the chevron, the rising and setting sun and stepped forms. It often has ornamentation based on Egyptian and Aztec cultures. Its original conception was most likely following the Paris 1925 exhibition where it demonstrated modernity, yet with links to historical discoveries of the time. Whilst Art Deco had a significant impact with ceramics, it was applied to all aspects of decorative art, furniture and architecture. It also impacted on fashion, graphic arts and industrial design.

Strangely, much of the Art Deco ceramic art that has caught my attention here at French flea markets has been English and, on occasion, American. This is because unlike the U.K, France was far more prolific in producing glass than ceramics and the likes of Lalique and Galle were important exponents of this art form. When it comes to clocks however, every flea market has at least two or three examples. Yellow- veined marble, veneered wood and strange elongated numerals immediately say French Art Deco, but quality is always excellent and together with the obligatory, or so it seems, garniture accompaniments, they certainly make a broad modernist statement.

Fig.245 Art Deco box with 1930/40s design elements

Fig. 246 Stylish 1930s coffee pot

Fig.247 The Madonna and child by Artibel. Dated 1938

CHAPTER 20

Architectural & Garden Antiques

The range of antique and vintage architectural items that can be found at any French flea market is vast and easily outstrips every other category of collectables.

In the 1960s, few demolition contractors and householders considered it worthwhile to salvage any unwanted or outmoded items. It was not until the 1970s when a boom in restoring property in a sympathetic manner to its period, that architectural salvage really took off. Even then, many interesting architectural salvage items were, because they had no practical use, ignored. Who at that time thought a rusty blue enamel French street sign would ever have decorative appeal?

For those with a large white van, French flea markets will be stocked with huge mirrors, stained glass windows, fireplace surrounds, pot-bellied stoves, doors, sinks and baths and much more. The average hunter however, will be looking for modestly sized items; perhaps light fittings, chandeliers or wall lights, curtain tiebacks and door fingerplates. Antique ironwork can be very decorative as can ornamental tiles and stucco work. In this category we include French enamel signs. Street signs are normally a wonderful shade of blue with white lettering, and the more unusual the name, the more appeal they give. Other signs are instructional, advertising or personal information. Vintage enamel signs have usually been exposed to changing weather conditions and as a result will have odd areas of rusting, but this is reassuring as it confirms the item is original vintage and not reproduction. In recent years there has been a great upsurge of interest in industrial salvage and now interior decorators are searching for stainless steel cabinets and tables, large light units, industrial seating and bulky industrial fittings. The end game is to 'up cycle' items for today's use in the domestic home as well as forward- looking commercial settings like trendy wine bars, hairdressers and boutiques.

Fig 248 Toleware wall candelabra.

Fig.249 Top section of very large stained glass panel

Fig.250 Iron hall light

Fig. 251 Pagoda lantern

Fig.252 Paris iron Balcony section

Fig.253 Elaborate iron doorbell around 1700s   Fig. 254 Ormolu finger plates.

Fig.255 Ormolu furniture mount

Fig. 256 Toleware wall light   Fig. 257 Ormolu door handles

Fig. 258 Cherub key escutcheon.

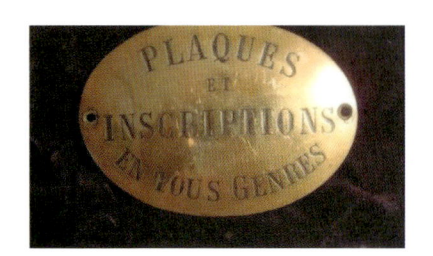

Fig.259 Ornate curtain rings.

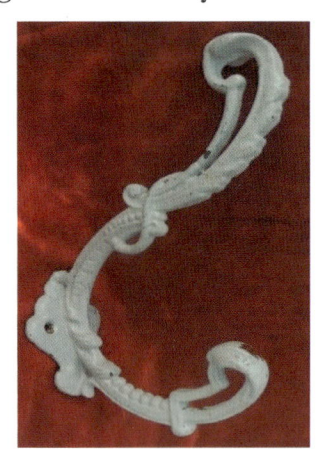

Fig. 260 Iron coat hook.

Fig. 261 Braided wool curtain tie-backs.

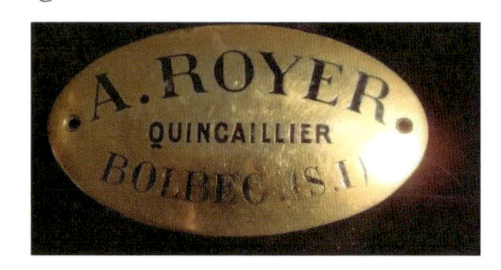

Fig. 262 Engraved brass shop signs.

130

Figs. 263 Various signs. Advertising, insurance and house numbers on enameled iron and Zinc etc.

Fig. 264 Large carved wood over-door architectural ornament

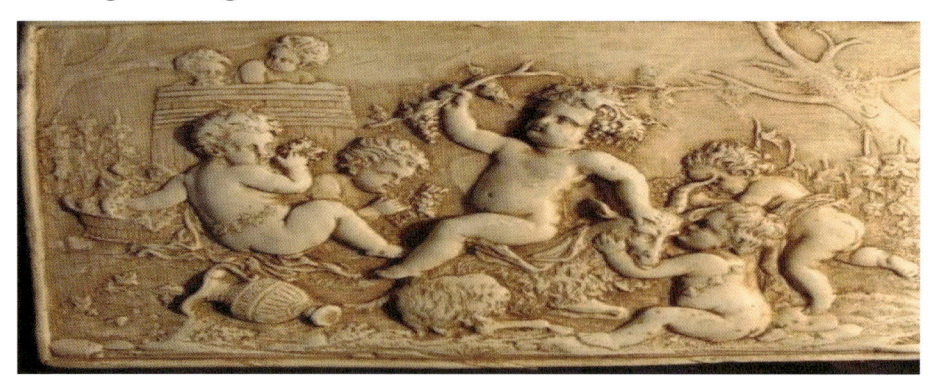

Fig.265 Stucco panel with nymphs making wine.

Fig. 266 19th century garden jardinière

Fig.267 Iron garden furniture around 1900

Fig.268 Hand-painted water can

Fig. 269 Wood and iron folding chairs 20th.century

Fig.270 Terracotta finial.

Fig. 271 19th century wood and iron wheel barrow

Fig.272. Wicker laundry baskets provide good and attractive storage

Fig.273 These days old leather suitcases are excellent architectural pieces.

CHAPTER 21

Kitchenalia and Household

Kitchenalia covers a whole field of collecting which is a treasure trove for cooking experts, the home kitchen and for display. From the most practical and well-crafted supplies like bread knives carved with a corn sheaf, bread boards giving thanks for our daily bread and coffee mills, to the more fanciful and attractive aspects of the kitchen, like tea towels and colourful racks and dishes.

Mortars and pestles are, perhaps, among mankind's longest surviving inventions in that their basic design has remained unchanged for two thousand years. Materials used throughout Europe ranged from glass, wood, marble, bronze and brass. The bronze mortar was the most common mortar in domestic use from the 16th to the 18th century where it was used for grinding herbs. In later years they were also used by pharmacies for the preparation of drugs. These early inverted bell-shaped mortars were often cast by bell founders, as bronze was the main material used. Over the centuries mortars became more decorative with bands of faunal and floral designs and handles and inscriptions that include the date and owners name as in the example in Figure 274. The wooden dairy bowl (Figure 281) is a very common find at markets. Some are comparatively small, whilst others can be quite enormous. The wooden porringer from the 16th century, Fig 280, is a rare survival which predated faience and pewter examples.

Top Tip

The majority of so-called antique mortars and pestles seen today are really 20th century reproductions. An original example will have a rich, but not necessarily dark patina and a network of striations from years of grinding substances between the mortar and heavy pestle. The bottom will also show signs of wear as it will have likely been rocked on a hard stone surface over a long period resulting in folded-over edges.

Fig. 274. Bronze mortar 1602   Fig. 275 17th century brass   Fig. 276 stone mortar

Fig. 277 Carved wooden bread boards, knives and spoons

Fig. 278 Hound carved on the end of a wooden spoon

Fig. 279 Enamel jugs, wire egg basket and tin milk crate

Fig.281 Wooden dairy milk bowl.

Fig. 280. Rare 16th century wood porringer

137

Fig. 282 18th19th century Brass and copper utensils

Fig. 283 19th century Normandy cider jug   Fig.284 Late 18th century harvest jug

Fig. 285 Cockerill iron.

Fig. 286 Wood and iron coffee mill

Fig. 287 Kitchen chalk board.

CHAPTER 22

Jewellery and items from the lady's boudoir

The word jewel originates from the old French word joule, and in France evolved into the French term for jewellery - bijouterie. Modern jewellery as we know it today can be classified as any small decorative item worn for adornment and refers as much to the delicacy of the workmanship as to the material value.

Since the dawn of time jewellery has been made from a vast range of materials and not only the obvious ones like gemstones, pearls, coral, amber and jet, but also beads made from stone or glass, shells collected from the sea and riverbank, even wood and root have been used to create what was often a status symbol. In the twenty first century, the list of possibilities is endless and includes plastics, metals and synthetic diamonds. Whilst today in Europe, items of adornment are mainly worn by women; this has not always been the case elsewhere.

In France, by the mid-1850s Paris asserted its role as the centre for luxury and this included jewellery to compliment the fashions of the time. The quality of French jewellery remains in the forefront of fashion accessory of the upper classes, even though styles have gone in and out of vogue. A rule of thumb when assessing value is the quality of the metal setting. It can be assumed that a platinum or high carat gold setting will contain a quality gem and will have been made by a good craftsman. Jewellery by the likes of Cartier are unlikely to be found at the average flea market, but many a good quality mass-produced 20th century jewel can be picked up. The quality of the setting will not be crucial; it will be the style of the period that will count for more. The cocktail or retro style from the 1940s brings a sudden frivolity with ballerinas and cartoon characters. By the 1960s plastic jewellery extended the possibilities incorporating shapes such as cats, foxes and ladybirds. The brooch on figure 290 is a typical collectable from the Paris designer Lea Stein.

For more than a century, France has been the centre for cultural exchange and so French jewellery is not in isolation from the rest of Europe, it is Worldwide.

Fig.288 Typical selection of European jewellery.

Fig. 289 Art Deco diamonds

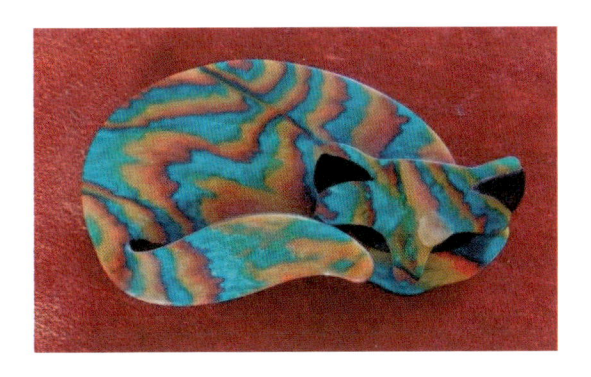

Fig. 290 1980s Plastic Lea Stein brooch

Fig.292. Jade and amber necklaces

Fig.291 Art Nouveau pendant

The most important components of the well-to-do French ladies boudoir were the bidet, the bed and the dressing room. The first task of the day would be her toilette which might be done by her servant, if she was wealthy enough to have one, or by herself, never by her husband. This grooming would only take place in her dressing room and not necessarily in private as it was quite customary for her to entertain visitors whilst carrying out her toilette. The term toilette comes from the French word toile which was a cloth that was placed over her shoulders while her hair was dressed.Sat at her dressing table she would admire herself in a large swing mirror as her servant toiled, often for some time, brushing her hair. She would also have small ornate pretty hand mirrors with matching brushes and containers for make-up and perfume. The toilette would not be complete without jewellery boxes and their opulence and quality of materials would reflect her standing.

With the industrial revolution in full swing, boxes of all types were produced in vast numbers for the newly emerging middle classes. Some would be small and suitable for a ring, others designed for a few items of jewellery, whilst large examples might have many compartments, fitted mirror, clock or musical box. The most commonly found caskets are the souvenir class. Mass produced in ormolu brass, they usually have clear glass sides and a local landmark on the lid.

Fig. 293 & 294 Crowns or tiaras in ormolu brass with paste stones. Mostly for young girls. Some of the small ones were made for Church statues.

Fig.295 &296 Jewellery caskets were highly ornamental and reflected the styles and tastes of the time. These are both mid to late 1800s.

Fig 297 & 298 Early ormolu photograph and picture frames were befitting of portraits of the upper-classes. The left hand portrait is painted on ivory.

143

She might also have pictures of herself. Perhaps a miniature painted on ivory and set in a frame, not too pretty, as an attractive frame might take an admirer's eye away from the beauty of her face. By the late 1800s, the photograph largely replaced the oil painting and industry turned out vast quantities of picture frames, mostly ormolu brass, but also in every kind of material to hand. But now, photograph frames were often, not always, but often much more elaborate, if fairly crudely produced. They almost always looked back to the past, using Rococo elements like great scrolls, cherubs and classical urns.

Fig.299 &300 Photograph frames for the less well-off appear to be just as ornate but were mass-produced, and thus of much inferior quality.

Fig.301 & 302 Mirrors fashioned in ormolu bronze and silver.

144

CHAPTER 23

Weapons, Warfare and Hunting

In France as with most parts of Europe, a wide range of ancient weapons from around the globe have found their way into everyday homes. Some brought back by distant relatives from Greek or Roman explorations and others from ethnic sources in Africa or Australasia. But what about the frequently seen prehistoric arrowhead and axe? These have undoubtedly been dug up from the back garden and rolling hills and valleys of prehistoric France. Two hundred thousand years ago and more, humans utilized and shaped tools and weapons by pressure-flaking stone with good fracture characteristics, including flint, quartzite, chalcedony, and jasper. One of the principal regions for survival of finds is around the Somme in northern France and in particular the site of Saint Acheul which gave its name to the Acheulean period (Figure 303).

Weapons of this period were limited to the arrow head, axe and spear. Swords can only be crafted through a forging process that had not been invented in the earliest phase of weapon construction, but by 2,000 BC, man had invented the metal weapon, at first in bronze and later in iron. These early and fairly primitive weapons were made primarily for hunting, but certainly by the Bronze Age period, man was using and developing weapons for protection and warfare. Sometimes there is a blurred distinction between ancient weapon technology and ethnographic survival. Peoples who, up until a few years ago, still made and used primitive weapons, are separated not only by geography, but also time scale as the example in Figure 304 Shows.
This example illustrates how the flint axe making technology from the prehistoric period, survived, and in some places remained, largely unchanged well into the early 20th century.

Weapons from the historic period are often enhancements of earlier weapon development. Early swords prior to the 18th century are rare and will almost never be seen at flea markets, but the 15th/ 16th century sword in Figure 305 was found at a fair and cost no more than 20 euros. Later swords and

Fig.303. Prehistoric Flint axe c.100,000BC

particularly those from the 19th century can often be found and despite the fact that their condition is invariably poor, they demand a relatively high price. Firearms are openly sold at fairs; they are usually sporting guns with stocks full of woodworm and of little interest, the exception perhaps being the English Joseph Manton gun I found at a fair in Southern France (Figure 307) which dates to around 1798-1800.

I have bought several cannonballs in France over the years. These solid iron projectiles were fired from cannon, without explosive charge, despite the fact that Hollywood always has them exploding on contact! The larger of the two illustrated, figure 308, has an interesting history.

At the commencement of the 'Hundred Years War' the English army landed at Saint-Vaast-la-Hougue, south east of Cherbourg on 12 July 1346, whereupon Prince Edward and several others were knighted in a nearby church at Quettehou before making their way to Caen. Almost seven hundred years later at a small flea market just outside Caen, a young boy of 10 or 11 was selling various bits and pieces and on his table he had a large cannonball. 'There was an old camp over there' he said pointing to a nearby field, 'I dug it up' he pronounced proudly and said he wanted 10 euros for it, which I willingly gave him.

Fig.304 Tribal art stone axe around 1900

Fig. 305 15th/ 16th century sword

Fig. 306 French short sword 1860/80

Fig. 307 English gun by Joseph Manton around 1800

With a weight of many kilos, the half mile walk back to my car was not without a little difficulty. However, research confirmed the site where he found it was likely to have been Prince Edwards's camp and the ball fits in with the story perfectly. The other one shown is 18th century and very much smaller.

Top Tip

As far as monetary value is concerned, cannon balls will generally have little value and the same goes for swords or firearms in poor condition. Condition plus rarity are the key words when it comes to value, but personally, I am more interested in their history. If you are prepared to accept examples in damaged or poor condition, then an interesting collection can be built, and for a minimal amount of expense.

Fig.308 Iron cannonballs. 14th century left. 19th century right.

Prisoner of war and Trench Art

Fig. 309 Engraved shell cases. 1917   Fig. 310 Plane made from bullets around 1940

The earliest items of prisoner of war art are the straw-work boxes from the Napoleonic period (Figure 324) and the wonderful bone ships and models, the latter rarely turn up today.

Throughout France, every flea market will have at least some items from world war 1, most passed down through the generations, and little regarded today. Such collectables are termed Trench Art. Although there is some evidence to show that trench art was made in the trenches by soldiers during the war, men on the front line often didn't have the time or tools to engrave the likes of spent artillery shells and so many were taken home and later engraved. Injured soldiers were also encouraged to do art work which included engraving and embroidery. Items most likely to have been made in the trenches were canteen objects, rings, letter openers made from bullets, lighters and inkwells, to mention just a few of the more common items.

Second World war collectables are also widely available throughout France, especially in towns along the Normandy coast associated with the D-day landings. The hand-made box in Figure 312 is particularly interesting as inside it has glass pictures of the prisoners family back home as well as his dog tag which tells us he was a prisoner at the German camp Stalag VA.

Fig. 311 Trench Art copper letter rack dated 1917

Fig. 312 WW2 French prisoner of war box with pictures of his family inside and 'dog tag' The box and identity tag made in Stalag VA 1943.

Although flea markets will often have the odd pieces, mainly shell cases, probably dug up locally, the main sales will be at fairs called Bourse Militaire. The items here were at the popular Sainte Mère- Eglise military sale.

CHAPTER 24

Miscellaneous and Curiosities

Fig. 313 Scandinavian 18th Century polychrome folk art carving

Miscellaneous and curiosities are a category which I define as interesting and unusual, mostly objects which do not readily fall into a specific category of collecting. They might be strange or they may have a bizarre aspect. Items in this category invariably have a diverse and disparate combination of materials and forms that provide glimpses of everyday life, not often represented by common artifacts.

The carved piece on Figure 313 is what is known as 'folk art': possibly from a Scandinavian fairground. It has a large hole in the centre, and forms just a small part of a larger section. The polychrome carving depicts primitive characters typical of the 18th/19th century. Another good example of true folk art is the stunning washing bat in Figure 314. It is whittled from a single piece of fruitwood and carved with a sailors' depiction of a mermaid holding an ornate letter M. Although the reverse has pared washboard ridges and has indeed been used, this type of bat is usually associated with sailor's love tokens and this is backed up by the letter M, presumably a girl's initial. Dating from circa 1800, it is a rare piece, but was bought for a very modest sum at a rural flea market and worth in excess of £400.

Fig. 314 Rare folk art washing bat. A sailors' love token made around 1800.

The green wax seal on Figure 315 came in its original round tin box. It is a Napoleonic seal and has the inscription LOUIS PHILIPPE ROI DES FRANCAIS, dated 1830.These are now quite rare due to their very fragile nature and although they are generally worth less than a £100, such pieces are very collectable today.

Fig.316 Carved wood folk art female head.

Fig. 315. Napoleonic seal of 1830

Fig. 317 17th /18th century carved wood Indian horse head with traces of polychrome.

Fig. 318 Dug-out cider mug. Note the incredible patina.

Fig.319 18th century plaster cast of Saint Catherine and child.

Fig.320 Arts and Crafts tile with aristocratic crest. It has the 'tree of life' springing out of the cup of plenty and two fine birds with family initials below.

Fig. 321. Pot with copy of Bayeux tapestry around 1900

Fig. 322 Silver filigree casket

Fig. 323 Wedding tiara stand.

Fig.324. Napoleonic prisoner-of-war straw-work box around 1800.

Fig 325 Bronze bird- form pin cushion

Fig. 326 Burmese archer in solid bronze. 1880s. 0.90 metre high.

Fig. 327 Persian Mamuluk Koran box

Fig. 328 large lion sculpture by Thomas Cartier, brother of the famous Jeweller.

CHAPTER 25

Ephemera, Toys and Games

Fig. 329 Calendar for 1875

Prior to the early 1800s, few items of a disposable nature were made and it was not until industrialisation began to impact on Europe that mass-produced goods began to appear. Suddenly, factories sprung up producing everything from fashion magazines with advertisements for the latest technology and products, to calendars, event programmes, tickets and souvenirs. This was the result of a sudden and growing demand for social interaction and new opportunities for mobility. Now we see the first postcards, greeting cards, pamphlets and posters, each reflecting the artistic trends of the period. The commodity market was not slow to cash in on this new way to advertise its products. Wine and food labels, boxes, cartons and tins, seed packets, soap, perfume and face powder boxes and their labels flooded the market. All of which were primarily designed to be discarded, but fortunately for us, many have survived to this day. It is also at this period when lithographic printing was cheaply available, that we see a sudden surge in games. The old traditional board games of chess and cards changed little, but now we see an inventive edge with new ideas and new takes on old favourites.

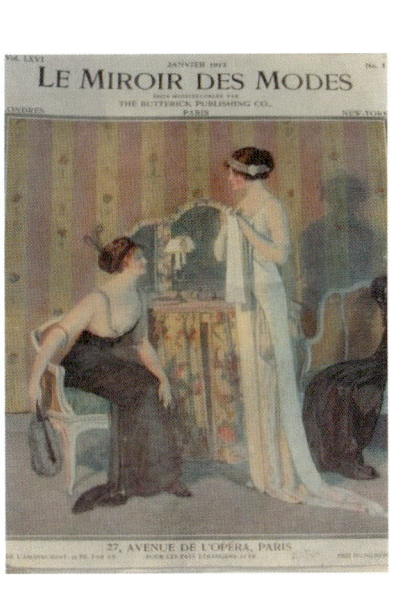

Figs. 330-331 1900s fashion plates.   Fig. 332 Music hall poster.

Fig. 333 Merchants shop bills

Fig. 334 Early greeting cards

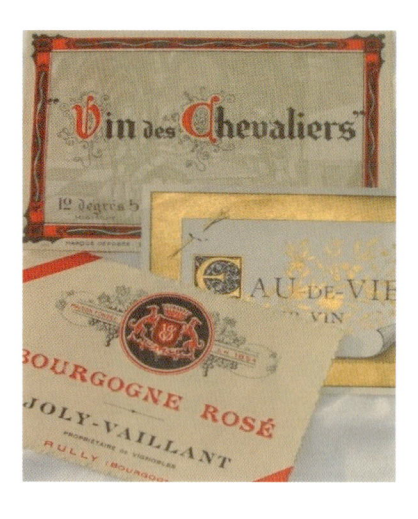

Fig. 335 Vintage wine labels

Fig. 366 cards of sewing accessories.

Fig. 377 Box of candles around 1890

Fig.338 Cardboard hat box

Fig.339 perfume box 1880s

Fig. 340. Decorative vintage soap box

Fig. 341 Vintage perfume bottle

Figs. 342 & 343 Wooden jigsaws 1900

Fig 344 Games compendium 1910

Fig. 345 Boxwood chess set

Fig. 346 Antique playing cards 1880s- 1920s

160

Soft toy teddy bears were first made by the German manufacturer Margaret Steiff in the 1880s and are distinguishable by the button in the left ear. So successful was the firm that by the early 20th century there were scores of makers, German toy manufacturers being the most prolific. The American soft toy company of Morris Michtom became famous as the maker of a bear named after President Theodore Roosevelt which became known as Teddy's bear. The rest is history.

Fig. 347. Antique bears and Steiff tiger. Early-mid 20th century

Fig.348 Early 20th century straw-filled rocking horse.

CHAPTER 26

Coins and Medals

A tin containing old coins can be found at most fairs, usually comprising low-value oddments left over from past holidays abroad. There will, inevitably, be quite a few pre- euro francs and maybe the odd coin passed down through the family. Most will have very little intrinsic value, but a quick rummage can sometimes prove worthwhile. People naturally think that Roman coins must be very valuable taking into account their 1,700 year age. Whilst a few and particularly those of gold or silver will have a good collector's value, the majority of brass, low- denomination issues can be bought for a mere euro or two. When it comes to historic coins, it is a strange fact that I have seen more English silver hammered coins here in France than French issues, but when it comes to the 17th century, French coins are more abundant, such as the silver ecu of 1652.(Figure 351). Napoleonic coins were made in vast numbers and are often seen, especially copper issues. Unless you have a good numismatic knowledge, it is probably best to leave well alone. There are rarities in French coins of the nineteenth and twentieth centuries, but once again specific targeted knowledge is required. Silver 5 and 10 franc pieces from the 1850s onwards are worth keeping an eye out for. They are often in remarkably good condition, but their value is primarily in their substantial silver weight and finesse. For the right price, buying silver francs can return a handsome profit.

Medals have been struck for centuries and comprise three distinct types; the war medal awarded for a military campaign, historical medals commemorating people or events and artisan medals such as those for agriculture, engineering or educational pursuits. Some like the Legion of Honour are awarded to both the armed forces and civilians. Others are decorations of a pure civilian or military character. Much like coins, this is a specialist subject and I only buy the odd medal for its decorative appeal.

Top Tip

I have on numerous occasions found British one and two pound coins mixed in with various foreign coins or even in tins of assorted buttons. These can usually be bought for far less than their face value. I once bought twelve pounds worth of English currency for 2 euros! Silver 5 and 10 franc coins will have a high silver value, so again they are worth looking out for.

Fig. 349. Roman coins from AD 54- 330

Fig. 350 Elizabeth I Hammered Silver Shilling 1584-6

Fig. 351 French Silver Ecu of Louis XIV dated 1652

Fig. 352 Medal of Jean Colberi. Minister of finance 1819-1883

Fig. 353 English silver medal Queen Victoria   Fig.354 Napoleon Bonaparte medal

Fig. 355 Plaque which accompanied the prestigious medal of honour. Caen 1913.

Appendix I

A rough guide to values.

From the outset, I was determined not to present this book as a price guide but as a starter tool for those wishing to spot the antique from the reproduction; the quality artisan created from the mass-produced, the sought after and rare from the common and undesired. Trends are continually changing and the internet has now made buying and selling antiques a global market. Within the course of a mere few months, the desirability of a class of antique can soar or fall dramatically, but certain factors remain fairly constant. Rarity and quality are the benchmark of world antiques, and not as some might imagine, age. A 2,000 year old Greek or Roman pot can be worth less than £100 and a 10,000 year old Mesolithic flint tool can demand little more than £10. Age added to scarcity however, can render an otherwise common item, most desirable.

Quality has always been the keyword for experienced dealers and collectors alike, and the age-old advice, buy the best you can, is ever more important today. This brings us to the vexed question of comparisons. Two comparable Worcester porcelain vases might look very similar, but to give them the same value could be a significant mistake. One might be painted by Harry Davies, an important landscape artist; the other perhaps by a far lesser artist or not signed at all. The expert will not miss the difference in quality. The better of the two could be worth ten times more than the similar article.

It is also a general rule that a true pair of items will be worth three to four times that of a single piece, and sometimes more.

Many of the examples in this book are not in perfect condition. In fact, some are far from it, but as a collector who is restricted by a budget, I would rather buy a rarity in damaged or worn condition than a common piece which can be picked up any day of the week. A good example of this is the 14th century octagonal pewter flagon (Figure 26) bought for a euro and despite a certain amount of damage; it still has some value, but in good condition it would be quite desirable and valuable.

Over the years, brass candlesticks have fluctuated greatly, but despite the ups and downs in demand, in this case, early equates to rare and subsequently to value. The Gothic candlesticks in Figure 12 were made between 1500 and 1550 and because of their age and rarity, are worth £500-£1,000. On the other hand the 19th century candlestick in Figure 16 is extremely common having been made in vast quantities and as a result worth little more than £30.

Figure 356 Poorly executed 18thcentury charger with weak interpretation.

Figure 357 Superb example of a Delft 17th century charger. Notice the difference in the crispness of the design

Quality of design and execution can also have an impact on value. Take for instance the two Delft chargers above. They are both interpretations of 17th century Chinese porcelain. At first sight they look quite similar, but when you look closer there is a vast difference between the two. The right-hand example, which is a hundred years earlier than the left, has a wide foliate rim with a design painted straight from a Chinese Wanli piece of porcelain from the 1600s. In contrast, the left hand example has a plain rim which has a confused interpretation of someone's idea of Chinese design. But it is the central panel which highlights the greatest difference between the two. The right hand example has two exquisitely painted deer which lifts its profile considerably from the later example which has a poorly executed basket of flowers. When it comes to value, the 18th century example on the left, might be worth £60 on a good day. The 17th century example on the right is worth £600-800.

I think it can be seen from the foregoing, that values are down to a good eye for quality, and knowledge of current market trends. There are many good books which specialize in antiques and their values, and whilst they can provide a useful guide, the prices are taken from auction house results from two years earlier. In that time, things change. I think a very good guide to antiques, collectables and their values, is via the internet. Sites such as ebay have an enormous selection of antiques for sale, and I believe, the prices those pieces fetch, will be a good indicator of their desirability and current market value. But remember, comparisons can be misleading. It is important to compare quality of execution, artwork, date and finally condition.

Appendix II

Glossary of Terms

A

Acanthus. Classical ornament of lapping leaves of the Mediterranean plant.

Acheulean. Paleolithic (old stone age) period named after St. Acheul, Amiens Northern France.

Alabaster. Soft gypsum rock used for carving, in particular, statues.

Anhua   Meaning hidden decoration. On Chinese porcelain it is un-coloured and only seen as impressions under a clear glaze. The decoration was carried out either by carving or incising.

Anthemion. Classical ornament in the form of a honeysuckle flower.

Antiquaire. Antique dealer also known as a marchand brocanteur.

Antiquité. French antiques shop selling high-end items.

Arcading. Continuous line of arches of medieval origin.

Armoire. A French term that loosely describes any type of wooden cupboard with or without shelves.

Art Deco. An international style that dominated architecture and the decorative arts from the mid-1920s until the start of the Second World War.

Art Nouveau. An ornamental style movement applied to the decorative arts across Europe and the United States from 1890-1910

Aumbry. A cupboard or secure receptacle which was inserted deep in the side wall of the sanctuary or sacristy of a Catholic Church.

B

Belle Époque. (Beautiful Era) was a period in French and Belgian history that began after the Franco-Prussian War in the late 1800s

Bentwood chair. First designed by Thonet in the 1850s. Furniture made out of glued and steam- bent wooden slats.

Black Forest. Wooden objects with carving that usually depict forest animals mainly bear, but also forest trees, branches, flowers and leaves. Many were German, but finest examples are attributed to master Swiss carvers.

Bourse Militaire Flea market sale dedicated to selling first and second World war memorabilia.

Braderie. Similar to the English jumble sale, traditionally where traders sell used clothing or objects outside or in a hall.

Brocante. Market stalls or shops selling second-hand goods which usually include antiques or collectables

Blanc de Chine. Chinese white porcelain from Dehua, mostly 18th/19th century.

C

Canton enamel. Chinese painted enamel, mostly on a copper base, originating from the port of Canton.

Chancay. People of the pre-Columbian Inca civilization of Peru.

Chinoiserie. European imitation of Chinese designs used principally on ceramics, fabrics and furniture. Usually portraying Chinese Mandarin characters, pagodas, river scenes and dragons. Gave rise to 18th century Rocco design. The example right is 18th century French Faience.

Chrémeau. Origins come from the chrism, which is oil mixed with balm and contained in a casket. Used for the sacraments of baptism.

Comptoise. A longcase clock with a swollen bellied, wood cabinet which originated in Morbier, in the French region of Comté.

Cloisonné. The application of enamels between thin metal compartments. Particularly popular in Japan during the 18th and 19th century.

D

Delftware. Tin-glazed blue and white or polychrome pottery made in and around the town of Delft in the Netherlands, also, generic term for similar.

Dépôt-vent. A shop or large warehouse whose purpose is to store items and sell them on behalf of dealers or individuals. The selling price is set by mutual agreement.

Dutch East India Company.(Vereenigde Oostindische Compagnie) A chartered company established in 1602, when the States General of the Netherlands granted it a 21-year monopoly to carry out trade activities in Asia. Pottery sometimes has the abbreviated monogram VOC

E

Ecu. French 18th century silver coin.

F

Faience. The French name for tin-glazed (Delft) pottery.

Flea market. French marché aux puces, sale of secondhand goods.

Flemish. The art and language of Flanders.

G

Girandole. A branched candleholder, usually backed by a mirror for reflection to increase illumination.

H

Hallmark. English system of stamped marks on silver verifying purity.

Hogscraper. Candlestick with a hog-scraper base. Named after its similarity to the hog scraper hair removing implement.

I

Icon. Religious image, mainly in paint or statue form and can be for secular or domestic use.

J

Jugendstil. Late 19th and early 20th century German decorative style parallel to Art Nouveau.

K

Kangxi. Chinese porcelain and art made during the reign of the Ch'ing dynasty Emperor Kangxi 1662–1722

Kraak porcelain. A category of Chinese export porcelain produced mainly during the Wanli reign until around 1640. It was among the first Chinese export wares to arrive in Europe in bulk quantities. It was copied by Delft and tin-glaze potters and exported in boats called carracks.

L

Lanthorn. An old word for lantern, a reference to the horn that once formed the panes.

Linenfold. A style of medieval relief carving used to decorate wood panelling. It is thought to imitate folded linen.

M

Maiolica. Italian tin-glazed pottery decorated in bright colours on a white background.

Mercury glass. A French product which was blown with silver mercury between layers to imitate silver.

Misericord. Decorative carved subject matter in wood under choir stall seat, often portraying heads and fanciful creatures, invariably allegorical.

Missal. Book containing the service for the mass. Early examples contained in highly carved wooden case.

O

Ogee. S- shaped curve in architecture and metal ware.

Oleograph. Process of reproducing oil paintings.

Ormolu. Gold coated bronze, used on furniture mounts.

P

Patina. Oxidized coating, usually green on copper-alloy metals. Also aged condition of wood, giving a highly glossy surface.

Pediment. Triangular, Greek-style gable on furniture.

Pewter. Alloy of tin and lead, used extensively for food and drinking utensils.

Poincon. French hallmark on silver. Before 1838, there were various marks that indicated fineness as well as place of manufacture but from 1838, French silver had two finesse levels: (1) 950 (95% silver) and (2) 800 (80% silver). The poinçon de garantie was the head of Minerva.

Porringer. Two-handled porridge or soup bowl.

Polychrome. Brightly painted pottery, terracotta, wooden furniture etc.

Pricket. Candlestick holder with spike instead of a socket.

Putti. The word originates from the Italian Putto meaning 'boy' sometimes called a cherub. Inspired by Renaissance Italy, they were made as decorative elements in all kinds of materials and in all parts of Europe and beyond.

Q

Quernstone. Stone, sometimes volcanic, used as a hand-mill for grinding corn.

R

Rat de Cave. French candlestick known as a Rat de cave, or cellar rat was used throughout France, originally in wine cellars lighting the room and checking the fermenting gases. These were simply made with turned fruitwood base and spiral iron shaft which has an internal stump which can be lowered or raised to control the height of the flame as the wick burns down. The handle or rats tail was ideal for carrying the light also to hang it on the edge of an oak barrel.

Reliquary. Container or shrine in which sacred relics are kept, usually the bones of a Saint.

Rococo. Artistic styles originating in France in the 18th century characterized by fanciful curved asymmetrical forms and elaborate ornamentation.

Romanesque. Architectural style from the mid-11th12th century.

Romayne. A style of 17th century ornamentation on furniture with carved human or grotesque heads.

Ruyi. Curled decorative object made of wood, jade, porcelain, ivory or precious metals that served as a ceremonial sceptre in Chinese Buddhism.

Rushlight. A simple lighting device consisting of a small bundle of rushes, 18 inches or so long which were dipped in used kitchen fat and inserted into an iron holder.

S

Salle de Vente. An auction room offering catalogued sales of antiques, works of art, collectables etc.

Sampler. Cross stitch or needlepoint alphabet done directly on fabric. Sometimes incorporating houses, trees and name and date.

Scarab. Egyptian frit-glazed pendant in the form of a sacred dung beetle.

Sleeper. Antique or collectable which has not been recognized for its potential value.

Slipware. Pottery that has been decorated with a coloured clay slip.

Spelter. Zinc-based metal used for forming statues and other cheap castings.

Spongeware. Pottery decorated with patterns, made by using a sponge to dab on coloured pigment.

Stele. Egyptian upright stone with sculpture and sometimes inscription.

Stirrup cup. Vessel of animal head form, handed to rider on horseback.

Stucco. Fine plaster wall coating moulded or sculpted into architectural decorations.

T

Teotihuacan. Mesoamerican culture from the city in central Mexico that flourished A.D 200–750.

Toile de Jouy. An off-white textile on which a repeated pattern depicting allegorical and pastoral scenes has been printed.

Toleware. Objects, often for the kitchen, made of tin that have been painted, japanned or lacquered with a picture or design.

Trench Art Objects made or decorated by soldiers, sometimes in the trenches during the first World war. Subjects were often love tokens for those back at home and were often made from shell-cases, bullets and oddments of copper and brass.

Tunbridgeware. True Tunbridgeware is decoratively inlaid woodwork using coloured rods, mostly on boxes. It was first developed in the spa town of Tunbridge Wells in Kent in the late 18th century. The term is often incorrectly applied to other forms of marquetry.

Touchmarks. Unique maker's mark stamped on pewter objects. May also include town and pseudo hallmarks.

V

Vente aux enchères d'antiquités.   Expensive, selective sale of quality antiques. Auction houses mostly situated in larger towns.

Vide greniers. Literally, 'empty your attic'. Equivalent to the English boot fair and basically the same as many flea markets.

W

Wanli.   Chinese Style and reign of the late Ming dynasty Emperor Wanli (1573–1620).

Washing bat.   Also known as a battledore. Wooden utensil used for beating clothes, sometimes decorated and given as a love token.

Wrigglework. Engraving of a metal surface with repeated zigzags to produce a pattern. Mostly employed in the 17th and 18th century.

Appendix III

Care and repair of antiques and collectables.

Metalwork

Before deciding whether to polish or not to polish a metal object it is necessary to determine the type of metal or combination of metallic elements. Copper and brass may have a dull gold tarnish or might be patinated green or dark brown. Some purists would do no more than clean with a soft cloth to slow down tarnishing, whereas I think most people would prefer a bright finish which compliments the colour of the metal. For this, use a good proprietary metal polish, but beware, overzealous rubbing will remove some detail, and over a period, can cause thinning of the metal. Bronze, on the other hand, should never be cleaned. An original dark brown or green patina is what gives bronze its unique look and any polishing will considerably lower its value both in aesthetic and monetary terms. Pewter, if left unpolished develops a matt grey finish which is generally considered highly attractive for antique pieces and requiring no more than a light brush and perhaps a gentle application of linseed oil or beeswax polish. There is a school of thought that advocates the polishing of Art Nouveau pewter, the argument being that at this period it was intended to be shiny and that the design elements work so much better when such pieces are silver-like. I think pewter was always intended to be bright in imitation of silver!

Silver very quickly develops a silky grey tarnish which does not damage the surface, in fact it protects it from corrosive elements and for some this is how silver should be left. As silver was intended to be bright and showy, it looks far better cleaned. Use a proprietary silver polish, but again, overzealous rubbing will blur detail, especially hallmarks and over time, reduce metal thickness. Silver plate will generally be recognised by its lack of hallmarks and tell-tale exposure of base metal.

There are many qualities of silver-plate some with triple plating others with a very thin layer of applied silver. The earliest examples are generally Sheffield plate which has a warm copper base.

By the 19th century the English firm of Elkingtons invented EPNS-electro-plated nickel silver. Cleaning will improve the appearance of silver-plate, but also invariably expose the base colour, especially on any raised or high points of detail. Other metals such as tin, lead and iron should only be washed in warm water, dried, and perhaps given a gentle wipe with a linseed oil rag. Repairs to metalwork can rarely be carried out successfully by anyone except an expert and will often leave an object disfigured and less desirable. The advice here is- only buy metalwork which is in the sort of condition which is acceptable without expensive repair. If it is, say, an early candlestick which is a bit dented and worn, that is part of its history, but if it has an ugly hole in the base where it was once converted to an electric lamp, then leave well alone.

Pottery and porcelain

Unlike metal ware, ceramics do not acquire a patina by exposure to oxidation, but may develop areas of crazing and browning. Most ceramics with a glazed surface can be safely washed in soapy warm water, but first check for any repairs as some types of glue will dissolve and repaired parts may come adrift. Delft and all tin-glazed faience will normally have areas of exposed body, particularly on rims and bases, so should be carefully wiped with a damp cloth and never immersed in water, in fact, any ceramics with unglazed body should be cleaned with care. When it comes to damaged pieces, deciding whether to repair or leave well alone, depends on the composition of the ceramic and the aesthetic values which it holds. Generally speaking, porcelain has to be perfect, collectors and dealers are unforgiving when it comes to damage. Pieces can be expertly restored, but at a cost! Country pottery and especially tin-glazed wares will invariably have areas of glaze flaking where the body is exposed. This is the nature of the material and considered acceptable providing it is not too extensive. Such wares should never be repaired or touched-up, they are far better left in their honest condition. Pottery and in particular, tin-glazed wares will often have rivets where early repairs have been carried out by itinerant smiths and are frequently almost invisible on the exposed surfaces. It is a matter of opinion as to whether such pieces should be purchased, but I do not have a problem and have bought items which would be far too expensive in perfect condition. I think this type of early repair is part of its history and shows someone else once valued the piece sufficiently enough to have it repaired.

Furniture

Antique furniture was not designed for modern day living. Humidity and sudden changes in temperature can cause wood to expand and contract and the greatest risk is from central heating which can result in warping. The effect of this can often be irreversible, but not necessarily evident at the time of purchase, so care is needed to inspect drawers, doors and less obvious elements. The quality of finish on wood, whether it be a piece of furniture or wood carving will greatly affect both its aesthetic appeal and value. An original patina must never be removed or cleaned with harsh abrasives. If the original finish is in good order, then a light wipe with a damp cloth will remove surface dirt. This should be followed by regular applications of beeswax polish. Woodworm is a significant problem in France and is rarely taken seriously by people selling infested furniture; they often consider the presence of all those tiny holes, a sign of great age. Even when told that a piece of woodwork has been treated, I do not accept it as necessarily true and will always treat items before introducing them into my home. Often, signs of woodworm are not immediately obvious. I turn articles upside down and give them a good tap. If this results in a heap of fine dust, then there is a problem somewhere within the piece of furniture. The treatment is quite simple; all parts should be thoroughly brushed over with insecticide fluid, making certain infected areas are heavily doused several times. It is worthwhile checking vulnerable woodwork at least twice a year.

Paintings, prints and manuscripts

These are all far beyond the average person when it comes to cleaning and repair and should be left well alone. A light brush will not hurt an oil painting, but a print might have unstable colour and foxing which can easily be moved across the image.

Jewellery

Items of jewellery are often made up from a variety of different elements; gold, silver, base metal and a multitude of different stones and settings. Cleaning antique jewellery is potentially a risky business unless you know what you are doing. A simple gold ring with a hard stone setting will probably come to no harm if immersed in warm soapy water, but must be dried scrupulously, preferably with the use of a hair dryer as moisture can get trapped behind a setting and cause corrosion. Soft and porous stones such as opals and pearls should never be exposed to immersion in water.

Textiles.

Any attempt to clean antique fabrics will almost always result in irreversible damage and should be left to an expert. A light brush or in some circumstances a gentle vacuum clean will often remove surface dirt without detriment to the fabric. Using nylon tights placed over the nozzle will prevent delicate material being sucked into the vacuum. A light spray with a fabric freshener will remove musty smells from old fabrics that are too delicate to wash. There are also proprietary solutions for removing iron- mould, but use these with care. First try a small area which is perhaps on an edge to make certain a detrimental effect will not be triggered.

Appendix IV

Selected Flea markets, Brocantes and Vide greniers.

Paris

Brocante des Abbesses

Clignancourt Saint-Ouen

Porte de Vanves

North

Amiens

Crevecoeur-le-Grand

Lille - La Braderie

Montreuil-sur-Mer

Maroilles

Central

La Haye-du-Puits

Le Mans (Trade only)

Lisieux

Saint-Michel-des-Andaines

South

Aix-en-Provence

Arles

Carpentras

Isle sur-la-Sorgue

Montpellier (Trade only)

Toulouse

Villeneuve-lès-Avignon

Béziers

South East

Annecy – Vieux Quartier

Dijon

For further details see the online calendar - brocabrac.fr

Appendix V

Common French bartering terms

How much is this please?	C'est combien s'il vous plait?
What is your lowest price?	Quel est votre prix le plus bas?
Would you accept 10 euro?	Accepteriez-vous dix euro?
It is too expensive for me!	C'est trop cher pour moi!
What is it for?	C'est pour quoi?
Does it have damage?	C'est endommagé ?
Has it been repaired?	Il a étré réparé?
Is it old or new?	C'est ancient ou nouveau?
Where did it come from?	D'où vient-il?
Do you know its history?	Vous connaissez son histoire?
Is it solid silver?	C'est l'argent massif?
Is it a painting or a print?	C'est une peinture ou une gravure?
It has lots of woodworm !	Il y a beaucoup d'vers du boi !
It is broken, what a pity.	C'est cassé, quel dommage
Thank you, I will think about it.	Merci, Je vais y réfléchir
Will you look after it for me?	Voulez vous garder pour moi?
Where can I get a good croissant and coffee?	Où est ce que je prendre un bon croissant et le café?

Appendix VI

French numbers and their pronunciation

Number		pronunciation
0	*zéro*	zay-ro
1	*un*	uh
2	*deux*	duhr
3	*trois*	twa
4	*quatre*	katr
5	*cinq*	sank
6	*six*	sees
7	*sept*	set
8	*huit*	weet
9	*neuf*	nurf
10	*dix*	dees
11	*onze*	onz
12	*douze*	dooz
13	*treize*	trez
14	*quatorze*	katorz
15	*quinze*	kanz
16	*seize*	says
17	*dix-sept*	dee-set
18	*dix-huit*	dees-weet
19	*dix-neuf*	dees-nurf
20	*vingt*	van
21	*vingt et un*	vant-ay-ur.
30	*trente*	tront
40	*quarante*	karont
50	*cinquante*	sank-ont
60	*soixante*	swa-sont
70	*soixante dix*	swa-son-dees
80	*quatre vingts*	kat-ra-van
90	*quatre vingt-dix*	kat-ra van-dees
100	*cent*	son
500	*cinq cent*	sank son
1000	*mille*	meel

INDEX

Alsace, 43

Altar cushion, 109

Antiquities, 5, 99

Architectural antiques, 126

Armoires, 71, 75

Art Deco, 6, 85, 113, 124, 125, 141, 169

Art Nouveau, 5, 6, 38, 85, 116, 117, 121, 124, 169, 172

Aumbry, 59, 169

Beadwork, 5, 105, 106

Belle Époque, 5, 119, 120, 122, 169

Beret, 114

Bible box, 79, 83

Black Forest, 87, 170

Boxes, 5, 79, 82

Bread boards, 135, 136

Breton pottery, 43

Bronze age flint arrowhead, 100

Calendrier Des Brocantes, 17

Candle box, 79

Candle stands, 75

Candle wall light, 127

Candlesticks, 20, 21, 22, 23, 24, 25, 50, 60, 167

Cannonball, 146, 148

Canton, 92

Ch'ing dynasty, 92

Chamber sticks, 23

Charolles, 43

Cherub, 54, 55, 56, 122, 173

Chess set, 160

Chest, 71, 79, 118

Chinese porcelain, 39, 167, 169

Chinoiserie, 91, 94, 170

Christofle, 38

Cider jug, 138

Clocks, 5, 85, 87

Cloisonné, 83, 170

Coffee pot, 34

Coins, 6, 162

Comptoise clock, 86

Costume, 108

Cradle, 73

Crucifixes, 60

Daum, 48, 120

Dauphiné., 55

Delft, 5, 39, 40, 46, 47, 167, 171, 172

Delftware, 29

Dépôt-vente, 17

Desvres, 43

Dowry sheets, 112

Drug jars, 40, 50, 51

Elkingtons, 38

Emile Galle, 48, 120, 123

Enamel signs, 126

Ephemera, 6, 156

Faïence, 5, 39

Fashion, 108, 112, 115

Fashion plates, 157

Finger plates, 129

Flea market, 5, 7, 9, 10, 11, 12, 14, 20, 27, 34, 49, 58, 60, 63, 71, 102, 108, 124, 126, 140, 146, 148, 151

Folk art', 151

Funerary stele, 100

Gallia ware, 38

Games compendium, 160

Girandoles, 77

Glass, 5, 24, 48

Greetings cards, 158

Hammered silver, 163

Harvest jug, 139

Hat box, 159

Haute Couture, 112

Hogscraper., 22, 23

Holy water stoop, 62

Hundred Years War', 146

Icons, 62, 66

Illuminated manuscript, 65

Iron doorbell, 129

Jardinière, 93, 123, 132

Jeanne d'Arc, 122

Jewelry box, 79

Jingdezhen, 90

Jugendstil, 116, 117, 172

Kangxi, 91, 172

Kitchenalia, 6, 135

Kraak-style, 39

Kutani, 94

La Galerie des Modes, 115

Lace, 108

Lalique, 48, 124

Lanterns, 5, 20, 24

Lea Stein., 140

Linenfold panels, 72

Lorraine region, 43

Luneville, 43, 45

Maiolica, 39

Majolica, 46

Manuscripts, 5, 64, 66

Medals, 162

Mercury glass, 50, 172

Milk crate, 137

Ming dynasty, 39, 176

Miniature, 63, 144

Mirrors, 77, 126, 142

Misericord, 63

Missal, 63

Monograms, 112

Mortars, 135, 136

Moustiers, 41

Mustards, 28

Napoleonic prisoner-of-war, 154

Neolithic saddle quern, 100

Nevers, 41, 82

New Caledonia, 103

Octagonal flagon, 27

Patch boxes, 79

Pewter, 5, 27, 118, 173

Picture frames, 38, 143, 144

Playing cards, 160

Polychrome, 41, 43, 54, 151

Porringer, 135, 138

Porringers, 28

Porte de Vanves, 10

Prickets, 20, 21

Quimper, 42, 44

Rat de cave, 22, 23, 173

186

Roman coins, 99, 162, 163

Roman pot., 101

Rouen, 41, 42, 46, 47, 66

Rushlight holders, 21

Rushlight,, 20

Ruyi sceptre, 96

Saint-Michel-des-Andaines., 12

Salacia, 188

Salle de Vente, 17, 174

Salts, 28, 34

Samplers, 5, 105

Sarreguemines, 43

Sewing box, 79

Shaft and globe, 48

Shop signs, 130

Silver, 5, 33, 35, 162, 163, 164

Snuff bottle, 96

Spelter, 120, 175

Sponge- ware, 44

Stained glass, 61, 126, 127

Steiff bears, 161

Stirrup cup, 34, 35

St-Ouen de Clignancourt, 10

Stucco panel, 132

Sun dial, 86

Swords, 145, 148

Table, 10, 13, 14, 15, 33, 41, 52, 71, 72, 74, 123, 142, 146, 148

Tankards, 34

Tea caddies, 79, 82

Textiles, 5, 108

Tie-backs, 130

Tin-glazed, 39, 46, 171, 172

Toile de Jouy, 109, 175

Toleware, 87, 175

Toys and games, 156

Tribal art,99, 102, 147

Trinket box, 79

Trundle beds', 76

Verification marks, 28

Vide grenier, 10

Villeneuve-lès-Avignon, 12

Wanli, 91, 167, 172, 176

Washing bat, 151, 152

Weapons, 6, 145	Wire egg basket, 137
Wedding tiara stand, 154	WMF, 117, 118
Westerwald, 45	Woodcarvings, 5, 53
White metal, 5, 33	Wooden jigsaws, 160
Wine bottles, 48	Wriggle- work, 29
Wine measure, 27	Writing box, 79

Figure 358 Silver gilt box with mythological Salacia- the female divinity of the sea.

NOTES

Printed in Great Britain
by Amazon